English for academic study:

C000065668

Reading & Writing

Source Book

John Slaght, Paddy Harben
and Anne Pallant

University of
Reading

CALS
Centre for
Applied Language Studies

Garnet
EDUCATION

Credits

Published by
Garnet Publishing Ltd.
8 Southern Court
South Street
Reading RG1 4QS, UK

First published 2006
This edition published 2009
Reprinted 2010

ISBN: 978 1 85964 518 5

British Cataloguing-in-Publication Data
A catalogue record for this book is available from
the British Library.

Production
Project manager: Simone Davies
Project consultant: Rod Webb
Editorial team: Simone Davies, Nicky Platt
Design: Mike Hinks
Illustration: Mike Hinks, Doug Nash
Photography: Corbis: Robert Essel NYC,
                    Jeremy Horner, Caroline Penn,
                    Michael Prince, Franco Vogt,
                    Roger Wilmshurst; Getty Images;
                    Mike Hinks; The United Nations.

Printed and bound in Lebanon by International Press:
interpress@int-press.com

The authors and publishers wish to acknowledge the
following use of material:

'Economics focus: On the move' © The Economist
Newspaper Limited, London (May 12th, 2001).

'Does Class Size Matter?' reprinted with permission.
Copyright © 2001 by *Scientific American*, Inc.
All rights reserved.

From Atkinson/Atkinson/SmithBem/Nolen-Hoeksema/
Harcourt, Inc. Hilgard's Introduction to Psychology, 12E.
(c) 1996 Wadsworth, a part of Cengage Learning, Inc.
Reproduced by permission. www.cengage.com/permissions

Middleton, N., 'Acid rain in Norway' in *Geography
Review*, Vol. 11, No. 4 (1998). Reprinted with
permission © Philip Allan Updates.

Everett, M., 'Impact – Skylarks in decline' in *Biological
Sciences Review*, Vol. 10, No. 2 (1997). Reprinted with
permission © Philip Allan Updates.

'Telemedicine comes home' reprinted with permission.
Copyright © The Economist Newspaper, London (2008)

Statistics Without Tears: A Primer for Non-Mathematicians
by Derek Rowntree (Penguin Books, 1982). Copyright ©
Derek Rowntree, 1982. Pages 14–21 reproduced by
permission of Penguin Books Ltd.

Common Questions about Climate Change
(pages 4–12), reprinted with permission © United
Nations Environment Programme and World
Meteorological Organization.

'The Global Village: Challenges for a Shrinking
Planet', reprinted with permission from *The Global
Village: Challenges for a Shrinking Planet* (*Understanding
Global Issues 98/7*).

'The New Linguistic Order' in *Foreign Policy*, Winter
1998–99 (pages 26–39), Joshua A. Fishman.

Contents

Text i-1: Economics focus: On the move

FINANCE AND ECONOMICS

The Economist, May 12th, 2001

Economics focus:
On the move

Economic analysis sheds light on the history of immigration and on its future

1949: Passengers at Cobh Harbour, County Cork, bound for Canada. Passage cost one hundred pounds.

During the spread of globalization in the three centuries leading up to the First World War, the migration of workers was consistently one of the biggest causes of economic change. Since 1945, the world has experienced a new era of globalization which is much quicker, and the international movement of labour is proving once again to be of the greatest significance. That is so despite the efforts of governments in richer countries to restrict migration, and despite basic changes in its economic nature. As a new study* by Barry Chiswick of the University of Illinois at Chicago and Timothy Hatton of the University of Essex makes plain, it is economic factors that have been the most important throughout the history of migration.

For many years after the discovery of America, the movement of free migrants from Europe was steady but quite small: transport costs were high, conditions harsh and the dangers of migration great. In 1650, a free migrant's passage to North America cost nearly half a year's wages for a farm labourer in southern England. Indentured work developed as a way around this. This meant that the workers were forced to work for their bosses for a period of time without pay. However, direct slavery dominated until the slave trade was stopped in the first half of the 19th century. By around 1800, North America and the Caribbean Islands had received some 8m immigrants. Of these, about 7m were African slaves.

The first era of mass voluntary migration was between 1850 and 1913. Over 1m people a year were attracted to the new world by the turn of the 20th century. Growing prosperity, falling transport costs relative to wages and lower risk all

Economic analysis sheds light on the history of immigration and on its future

pushed in the same direction.

Between 1914 and 1945, war, global depression and government policy helped to reduce migration dramatically. During some years in the 1930s, people returning to Europe from the United States, even though comparatively few, actually outnumbered immigrants going the other way – a rare case for America of net emigration.

After the Second World War, the economics of migration reasserted itself. The cost of travel fell steeply. But now the pattern changed. Before long, Europe declined as a source of immigration and grew as a destination. Emigration from developing countries expanded rapidly: incomes there rose enough to make emigration feasible, but not enough to make it pointless. Many governments began trying to control immigration. The numbers of legal and illegal immigrants grew nonetheless, as economics had its way.

Winners and losers

Migration, it is safe to assume, is in the interests of (voluntary) migrants; they would not move otherwise. The evidence suggests that it is also very much in the overall interests of the receiving countries. But, as Chiswick and Hatton point out, there are losers in those countries. The increase in the supply of labour presses down the wages of competing workers, at least in the first instance. (Later, as the stock of capital grows in response, that effect may be partially reversed.)

The economic conditions now seem favourable for an enormous further expansion of migration. On the face of it, this will be much like that of a century ago. As before, the main expansionary pressures are rising incomes in the rich countries and rising incomes in the poor ones. (This second point is often neglected: as poor countries get a little less poor, emigration tends to increase, because people acquire the resources to move.) The study emphasizes, however, two crucial differences between then and now.

One is that, in the first decade of the 20th century, the receiving countries needed lots of unskilled workers in industry and farming. In the first decade of the 21st century, in contrast, opportunities for unskilled workers who can migrate are decreasing. In America, wages of unskilled workers are falling, in absolute as well as relative terms. The fall is enough to hurt the workers concerned, but not to deter new immigrants. Several studies suggest that immigration has made a definite contribution to this decline.

And the other big difference between now and a century ago? It is that the affected rich-country workers are in a stronger position to complain, and get something done. The most likely result is that a trend that is already well established (either as explicit policy or customary practice) will continue; countries will try to restrict the immigration of unskilled workers, giving preference to workers with skills.

This does help, in one way, quite apart from reducing the skills deficit in rich countries; it eases the downward pressure on wages at the bottom. However, the idea has disadvantages too. It turns away many of the poorest potential migrants, which is hard to justify in humanitarian terms. Also it pushes others from this group into illegal immigration, which exposes them to dangers, makes assimilation more difficult and may even cause a stronger downward pull on the wages of some low-skilled workers in receiving-countries than the legal entry of the same migrants.

On top of all this is the skills drain from the sending countries. Already some of the world's poorest nations lose almost all the doctors they train to jobs in Europe or North America. Financial remittances offset some of that loss, but not all.

Today's migration, much more than the migration of old, causes some insoluble problems. Regard for individual freedom argues for a more liberal immigration regime in the rich countries, and for unskilled migrants as well as skilled ones. With or without such a regime, more migrants are coming. And in either case, the question of compensation for the losers, in rich countries and poor countries alike, will demand some attention.

*Chiswick, Barry R. and Hatton, Timothy J. (August 2002) 'International Migration and the Integration of Labour Markets', ftp://repec.iza.org/RePEc/Discussionpaper/dp559.pdf

Source: On the move. (2001, 12 May). [Electronic version]. *Economist*, 359(8221), 78.

Text 1-1: The influence of class size on academic achievement

THE INFLUENCE OF CLASS SIZE ON ACADEMIC ACHIEVEMENT

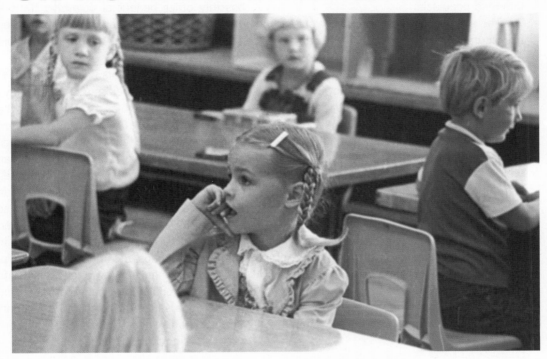

Education is a pillar of modern society and the subject of endless, often passionate arguments about how it can best be improved. In the U.S., there is heated
5 debate following revelations that the country's secondary school students perform poorly relative to many Asian and European students. The news coincided with increasing concern over the nation's urban and
10 lower-income suburban schools, too many of which are languishing at achievement levels far below those of middle-class and upper middle-class suburban schools.

Of all the ideas for improving education,
15 few are as simple or attractive as reducing the number of pupils per teacher. With its uncomplicated appeal and lack of a big, powerful group of opponents, class-size reduction has lately developed from a sub-
20 ject of primarily academic interest to a key political issue. In the United States, more than 20 states and the federal government have adopted policies aimed at decreasing class sizes, and billions of dollars have been
25 spent or committed in the past few years. The demand for smaller classes is also growing in Canada, Australia, the United Kingdom, and even Japan, whose record of secondary school performance is the envy of
30 most other developed countries.

The most obvious drawback to class-size reduction is the huge cost. It requires more teachers, more classrooms and more classroom equipment and resources. These
35 expenses can dwarf the price of alternative schemes, such as testing teachers or increasing their pay as a means of attracting better candidates. The state of California, for example, has been spending more than
40 $1.5 billion annually over the past several years to reduce class size to 20 or fewer for children in the four- to seven-year-old bracket. On the other hand, if smaller classes really do work, the economic benefits could be huge.

45 They would accrue not just from the benefits of a better-educated workforce but also from other sources, such as the avoided medical costs and sick days of a healthier, more informed populace.

50 The surge of interest in smaller classes has spurred fresh analyzes of the largest, most conclusive study to date, which took place in Tennessee in the late 1980s. At the same time, new data are flowing from 55 various initiatives, including the California programme and a smaller one in Wisconsin. These results and analyzes are finally offering some tentative responses to the questions that researchers must answer before 60 legislators can come up with policies that make educational and economic sense: Do small classes in fact improve school achievement? If they do, at what age-level do they accomplish the greatest good? What kind of 65 students gain the greatest benefit, and most importantly, how great is the benefit?

WHAT ARE THE BENEFITS OF SMALLER CLASS SIZES?

Educators have a multitude of explanations 70 for why smaller class sizes might be expected to improve academic performance, although frequently the ideas are anecdotal. Fewer students in the classroom seem to translate into less noise and disruptive 75 behaviour from students, which not only gives the teacher more time for class work but also more freedom to engage students creatively – by, for example, dividing them into groups for specific projects. In addition, 80 smaller classes make it more likely that the teacher can give greater individual attention to struggling students. Smaller classes also allow teachers to encourage more discussion, assign more writing and closely exam- 85 ine their students' written work. In other words, much of the benefit of reduced class size may depend on whether the teachers adapt their methods to take advantage of

smaller classes. Finally, some analysts 90 believe that the very youngest age group in smaller classes are more likely to develop good study habits, higher self-esteem and possibly other beneficial cognitive traits – which may very well persist for years, even 95 after the students have gone back to more normal-sized classes.

One way investigators have attempted to analyze the effects of class size is by reviewing existing data, such as records kept by the 100 U.S. Department of Education. These show that between 1969 and 1997, the average number of pupils per teacher in American public and private elementary schools fell from 25.1 to 18.3, a decline of greater than 105 27%. In secondary schools, the number also fell, from 19.7 to 14.0. Of concern, however, is the fact that despite these steep drops in pupil-teacher ratios, the improvement in academic performance was negligible. Data 110 from the National Assessment of Educational Progress – a series of tests that is the only United States-wide indicator of student knowledge in reading, mathematics, science and other subjects – show no significant 115 gains. In some specific age and subject categories, such as 17-year-olds and science, performance actually decreased slightly.

WHAT THE RECORD SHOWS

However, these findings do not necessarily 120 mean that class size makes no difference. For a variety of reasons, most researchers, including the writers, pay little attention to these figures (Figure 1). For instance, schools strive for more than just high test 125 scores; they also usually try to keep their dropout rate low. In fact, the dropout rate for students aged 16–24 fell from 15 to 11 per cent over the period. Because dropouts generally come from the low end of the 130 achievement distribution, a reduction in dropout rate could be expected to pull down average test scores in the upper grades.

FIGURE 1: MILESTONE STUDIES IN CLASS SIZE

PROJECT	STATE	STUDENTS PARTICIPATING	APPROX. COST	SMALL CLASS SIZE	KEY FINDINGS
STAR 1985–89	Tennessee	10,000	$12m	13–17	Significant performance benefit of 0.2 standard deviation; larger gains for minority pupils
Class size reduction	California	1.8m	$5 billion	Less than 20	Small performance gain of about 0.05 to 0.1 standard deviation; no greater gains for minorities
SAGE	Wisconsin	64,000	£.03m	12–15	Significant performance advantage of 0.2 standard deviation; larger gains for minority pupils

Another reason for discounting these data goes right to the heart of the difficulties 135 in this field of study: it is hard to isolate the effects of class size from the myriad factors that influence student performance. The reality is that in 1995 only 68% of American students came from families with 140 two parents in the home – down from 85% in 1970. The fraction of children who had difficulty speaking English rose from 2.8% in 1970 to 20.2% in 1995. There was some good news: the median level of education 145 among parents increased slightly during that time period, as did the level among teachers, whose average amount of experience also went up.

Basically, demographic shifts make it 150 very difficult to assess the effect of reductions in pupil–teacher ratios. Well-designed experiments attempt to cancel out the influence of those other factors by randomly assigning students and teachers 155 to different class sizes and by including a large sample. Over the past 35 years, hundreds of studies and analyses of existing data have focused on class size. Most found evidence that smaller classes 160 benefit students, particularly at the youngest level, and especially children in danger of becoming underachievers.

Unfortunately, most of these studies were poorly designed. Teacher and student 165 assignments were rarely sufficiently random; a number of studies were simply too brief or too small, and too few had independent evaluation. The notable exception was the Tennessee study. The distinguished 170 Harvard University statistician, Frederick Mosteller, has called it 'one of the greatest experiments in education in United States history'. The Student–Teacher Achievement Ratio, better known as Project STAR, was a 175 state-sponsored, $12 million demonstration programme (see Figure 1). Students entering kindergarten were randomly assigned to one of three kinds of classes: a small class of 13 to 17 children, a 180 normal-sized class of 22 to 26 children, or a normal-sized class with both a teacher and a full-time teacher's assistant. The students remained in whatever category they had been assigned to until they had 185 reached the third grade, after which they joined a normal classroom in the fourth. To ensure that teaching quality did not differ, teachers were randomly assigned to small and normal-sized classrooms. Few 190 teachers received any special training for working with small classes, and there were no new curricular materials.

A CASE STUDY: SHINING STAR

After the study ended in 1989, researchers conducted dozens of analyzes of the data. One of the few points analysts agree on is that the teacher's assistants did not make any differ-
5 ence to academic performance. Researchers disagree about how long students have to be in smaller classes to get a benefit, how big that benefit is, when it becomes noticeable – in other words, the collected findings have
10 yielded no consensus on the issues of real interest to policymakers.

Jeremy Finn of the State University of New York and Charles M. Achilles of Eastern Michigan University found 'an array of
15 benefits of small classes' in their review. Finn calculated that students in the small classes outperformed their counterparts in normal-sized classes by a fifth of a standard deviation, and that this sizable jump in achievement
20 generally appeared by the first grade. Best of all, this advantage seemed to persist into upper elementary levels even after students returned to larger classes. In order to appreciate how big a difference there is in terms of a fifth
25 of a standard deviation, it is necessary to compare two pupils first starting school who are as average as it is possible to be statistically. Both are in the 50th percentile, meaning that half of the other pupils perform better than
30 those two and that half perform worse. One student should be placed in a small class, and the other in a normal-sized class. After a year, the pupil in the small class will be in the 58th percentile – in other words, the student will be
35 doing better than nearly 60% of his or her peers – while the other student will still be doing better than only 50%. Finn and Achilles also found that the effect was stronger for ethnic minority students, by a factor of two

40 or three. In other words, black or Hispanic children improved by two-fifths to three-fifths of a standard deviation – a significant finding from a policy point of view, because minorities typically score about one standard deviation
45 below their peers on standard tests.

A few analysts, notably Eric Hanushek of Stanford University's Hoover Institute, criticize STAR and some of the key conclusions reached by its proponents. Hanushek agrees
50 that students can gain an initial benefit from small classes. But, he argues, the STAR data cannot be used to prove that the gains persist for years after a student has returned to normal-sized classes. If a child is still doing
55 well years later, it is hard to know how much of the performance stems from other factors, such as a supportive home. Hanushek also disagrees with an analysis indicating that the benefits of small classes accumulate – that
60 students who stay in such classes for several years widen the performance gap with their peers in large classes year by year. When he studied the four-year gains of STAR students who were in smaller classes from kindergarten
65 until they reached grade three, he did not find the gains to be larger than those logged in kindergarten. He and others have also shown that during the study, too many children migrated from the regular to the small classes,
70 probably because school personnel caved in to parental demands. Hanushek further asserts that STAR had insufficient checks to ensure good randomization of teacher and student placement in classes. These are good points,
75 but they do not really undermine the findings of STAR of a statistically significant benefit of being in a class of between 13 and 17, rather than 23, students.

The Authors: RONALD G. EHRENBERG, DOMINIC J. BREWER, ADAM GAMORAN and J. DOUGLAS WILLMS collaborated on a paper surveying studies of class size and academic performance for the May 2001 issue of *Psychological Science in the Public Interest*. Ehrenberg is the Irving M. Ives Professor of Industrial and Labour Relations and Economics at Cornell University and the author of *Tuition Rising: Why College Costs So Much* [Harvard University Press, 2000]. Brewer, who specializes in the economics of education, is the director of Rand Education, which analyzes programmes and policies on education issues, and is a visiting professor of economics at the University of California, Los Angeles. Gamoran, a former Fulbright scholar, is a professor of sociology and education policy studies at the University of Wisconsin – Madison. Willms is a professor of the Canadian Research Institute for Social Policy at the University of New Brunswick.

Source: Ehrenberg, R.G., Brewer, D.J., Gamoran, A. & Willms, J.D. (2001). Does class size matter? [Electronic version]. *Scientific American*, 285(5), 78-85

Text 1-3: The Asian paradox: Huge classes, high scores

THE ASIAN PARADOX
HUGE CLASSES, HIGH SCORES

BY GLENN ZORPETTE

Study after study ranks schoolchildren in Japan and other developed Asian countries among the best in the world, particularly on standardized tests of 5 mathematics and science. American high school students, meanwhile, have slipped somewhere below those in Greece, Lithuania, Taiwan and Singapore in advanced mathematics 10 and science. However, classes in Asia are large; forty students for one teacher would be normal in most of the region. In contrast, elementary school class sizes in the United States average about 15 24, according to the U.S. Department of Education.

The question is why Asian children do so well in such large classes. In Japan, for example, the discipline is legendary. 20 Such discipline is not imposed by fearsome teachers, according to Catherine Lewis, an expert on the Japanese educational system and a senior researcher at Mills College. Instead, 25 students are honoured to be chosen to lead lessons, and they take turns calling the class to order, experiencing firsthand what it is like to quieten down an unruly group of students. As a result, teachers 30 manage the class by relying on 'the cumulative general power of self-reflection, rather than by punishing and rewarding,' Lewis explains. Japanese teachers and students also spend much 35 more time together – the usual year is about 40 days longer than in the United States – and more time bonding with one another at school festivals and on field trips and hikes. 'There's an incredibly 40 strong emphasis on class, group and school being meaningful entities for the children,' Lewis says. Japan's prowess in academic achievement is also sustained by something it does not have: ethnic 45 and linguistic diversity. Finally, Asian parents are far less likely than Americans to be divorced and are more likely to be involved in their children's education.

The downside of the Asian system is 50 that the rigid national standards do not do much to foster creativity. At the same time, in Japan some children strive hard to excel partly because they become burdened early on by the fear of failing. 55 Given the deep cultural differences, it is not clear which parts of the Asian formula could work in other countries such as America. However, the Asian experience does demonstrate what can 60 be done when discipline grows from the bottom up. In that kind of environment, elementary school teachers can focus on 'creating happy memories', as one Japanese teacher described her main 65 purpose to Lewis.

Glenn Zorpette is a writer based in New York.

Source: Zorpette, G. (2001). The Asian Paradox. In R.G. Ehrenberg, D.J. Brewer, A. Gamaran, & J.D.Willms, Does class size matter? [Electronic version]. *Scientific American*, 285 (5), 78-85

Early human development

Interaction between nature and nurture

A The question of whether heredity ('nature') or environment ('nurture') is more important in determining the course of human development has been debated through the centuries. For example, the
5 seventeenth-century British philosopher John Locke rejected the prevailing notion of his day that babies were miniature adults who arrived in the world fully equipped with abilities and knowledge and who simply had to grow in order for these inherited characteristics
10 to appear. On the contrary, Locke believed that the mind of a newborn infant is a 'blank slate' (*tabula rasa*). What gets written on this slate is what the baby experiences – what he or she sees, hears, tastes, smells and feels. According to Locke, all knowledge comes to us
15 through our senses. It is provided by experience; no knowledge or ideas are built in.

B The advent of Charles Darwin's theory of evolution (1859), which emphasizes the biological basis of human development, led to a
20 return of the hereditarian viewpoint. With the rise of behaviourism in the twentieth century, however, the environmentalist position once again gained dominance. Behaviourists such as John B. Watson and B.F. Skinner argued that
25 human nature is completely malleable: early training can turn a child into any kind of adult, regardless of his or her heredity. Watson stated the argument in its most extreme form: 'Give me a dozen healthy infants, well-formed, and
30 my own specified world to bring them up in, and I'll guarantee to take any one at random and train him to be any type of specialist I might select – doctor, lawyer, artist, merchant-chief, and yes, beggar-man and thief, regardless of his
35 talents, penchants, tendencies, abilities, vocations, and race of his ancestors' (1930, p.104).

C Today most psychologists agree not only that both nature and nurture play important roles but that they interact continuously to guide development.
40 For example, we shall see in Chapter 12 that the development of many personality traits, such as sociability and emotional stability, appear to be influenced about equally by heredity and environment; similarly, we shall see in Chapter 15
45 that psychiatric illnesses can have both genetic and environmental determinants.

D Even development that seems most obviously to be determined by innate biological timetables can be affected by environmental events. At the
50 moment of conception, a remarkable number of personal characteristics are already determined by the genetic structure of the fertilized ovum. Our genes program our growing cells so that we develop into a person rather than a fish or
55 chimpanzee. They decide our sex, the colour of

Early human development

our skin, eyes, and hair and general body size, among other things. These genetic determinants are expressed in development through the process of maturation – innately determined
60 sequences of growth and change that are relatively independent of environmental events.

E For example, the human fetus develops within the mother's body according to a fairly fixed time schedule, and fetal behaviour, such as
65 turning and kicking, also follows an orderly sequence that depends on the stage of growth. However, if the uterine environment is seriously abnormal in some way, maturational processes can be disrupted. For example, if the mother
70 contracts German measles during the first three months of pregnancy (when the fetus's basic organ systems are developing according to the genetically programmed schedule), the infant may be born deaf, blind or brain-damaged,
75 depending on which organ system was in a critical stage of development at the time of infection. Maternal malnutrition, smoking, and consumption of alcohol and drugs are among the other environmental factors that can affect
80 the normal maturation of the fetus.

F Motor development after birth also illustrates the interaction between genetically programmed maturation and environmental influence. Virtually all children go through the same sequence of
85 motor behaviours in the same order: rolling over, sitting without support, standing while holding on to furniture, crawling, and then walking. But children go through the sequence at different rates, and developmental psychologists began
90 very early in the history of the discipline to ask whether learning and experience play an important role in such differences.

G Although early studies suggested that the answer was no (McGraw, 1935/1975; Dennis & Dennis,
95 1940; Gesell & Thompson, 1929), more recent studies indicate that practice or extra stimulation can accelerate the appearance of motor behaviours to some extent. For example, newborn infants have a stepping reflex; if they are held in
100 an upright position with their feet touching a solid surface, their legs will make stepping movements that are similar to walking. A group of infants who were given stepping practice for a few minutes several times a day during the first two
105 months of life began walking five to seven weeks earlier than babies who had not had this practice (Zelazo, Zelazo & Kolb, 1972).

H The development of speech provides another example of the interaction between genetically
110 determined characteristics and experience. In the course of normal development, all human infants learn to speak, but not until they have attained a certain level of neurological development; no infant less than a year old
115 speaks in sentences. But children reared in an environment in which people talk to them and reward them for making speechlike sounds talk earlier than children who do not receive such attention. For example, children reared in
120 middle-class American homes begin to speak at about one year of age. Children reared in San Marcos, a remote village in Guatemala, have little verbal interaction with adults and do not utter their first words until they are
125 over two years old (Kagan, 1979).

Capacities
of the newborn

A At the end of the nineteenth century, psychologist William James suggested that the newborn child experiences the world as a 'buzzing, blooming confusion', an idea
5 that was still prevalent as late as the 1960s. We now know that newborn infants enter the world with all sensory systems functioning and are well prepared to learn about their new environment.

B Because babies cannot explain what they are doing or tell us what they are thinking, developmental psychologists have had to design some very ingenious procedures to study the capacities of young infants. The basic method
15 is to introduce some change in the baby's environment and observe his or her responses. For example, an investigator might present a tone or a flashing light and then see if there is a change in heart rate or if the baby turns its
20 head or sucks more vigorously on a nipple. In some instances, the researcher will present two stimuli at the same time to determine if infants look longer at one than the other. If they do, it indicates that they can tell the stimuli apart and
25 may indicate that they prefer one to the other.

Vision

C Because the visual system is not well developed at birth, newborns have poor visual acuity, their ability to change focus is limited, and they are very
30 nearsighted. An adult with normal vision is said to have 20/20 vision; a nearsighted adult with 20/30 vision is able to see at 20 feet what an adult with normal vision can see at 30 feet. Using this same index, a newborn has 20/660 vision. At six
35 months this has improved to 20/100; and by two years, the child can see almost as well as an adult (Courage & Adams, 1990).

D Despite their visual immaturity, newborns spend a lot of time actively looking about. They scan the
40 world in an organized way and pause when their eyes encounter an object or some change in the visual field. They are particularly attracted to areas of high visual contrast, such as the edges of an object. Instead of scanning the entire object, as an adult
45 would, they keep looking at areas that have the most edges. They also prefer complex patterns to plain ones, prefer patterns with curved lines to patterns with straight lines, and they are especially interested in faces (Franz, 1961). In an experiment on 'visual
50 preferences', newborns as young as 10 hours to five days old were shown disks that differed in particular ways – a face like a circle, a bull's-eye, an array of fine print, and disks coloured white, yellow or red. Infants could tell the difference between them and looked
55 at different patterns for different lengths of time.

E The possibility that there is an inborn, unlearned preference for faces initially aroused great interest, but later research showed that infants are not attracted to faces *per se* but to stimulus characteristics such as
60 curved lines, high contrast, interesting edges, movement and complexity – all of which faces possess (Banks, Salapatek, 1983; Aslin, 1987). Newborns look mostly at the outside contour of a face, but by two months they focus on the inside of the face – the
65 eyes, nose and mouth (Haith, Bergman, & Moore, 1977). At this point parents notice with delight that the baby has begun to make eye contact.

Text 2-3: Hearing, taste and smell

Early human development

Hearing, taste and smell

F Newborn infants will startle at the sound of a loud noise. They will also turn their heads toward the source of a sound. Interestingly, the head-turning response disappears at about six weeks and does not reemerge until three or four months of age, at which time the infants will also search with their eyes for the source of the sound.

G The temporary disappearance of the head-turning response probably represents a maturational transition from a reflexive response controlled by subcortical areas of the brain to a voluntary attempt to locate the sound source. By four
10 months, they will reach in the correct direction toward the source of sound in the dark; by six months, they show a marked increase in their responsiveness to sounds that are accompanied by interesting sights and are able to pinpoint the
15 location of sound more precisely, an ability that continues to improve into their second year (Hillier, Hewitt & Morrongiello, 1992; Ashmead *et al.*, 1991; Field, 1987).

H Newborn infants can also detect the difference
20 between very similar sounds, such as two tones that are only one note apart on the musical scale (Bridger, 1961), and they can distinguish sounds of the human voice from other kinds of sounds. We will see in Chapter 9 that they can also
25 distinguish a number of critical characteristics of human speech. For example, one-month-old infants can tell the difference between such similar sounds as 'pa' and 'ba'. Interestingly, infants can distinguish between some speech sounds better
30 than adults. These are sounds that adults 'hear' as identical because they are not distinguished in their native language (Aslin, Pisoni & Jusczyk, 1983). By six months of age, the child will have picked up enough information about the
35 language that it will also have begun to 'screen out' sounds it does not use (Kuhl *et al.*, 1992). Thus, human infants appear to be born with perceptual mechanisms already tuned to the properties of human speech that will help them
40 in their mastery of language (Eimas, 1975).

I Infants can discriminate differences in taste shortly after birth. They prefer sweet-tasting liquids to those that are salty, bitter, sour or bland. The characteristic response of the newborn to a
45 sweet liquid is a relaxed expression resembling a slight smile, sometimes accompanied by lip-licking. A sour solution produces pursed lips and a wrinkled nose. In response to a bitter solution, the baby will open its mouth with
50 the corners turned down and stick out its tongue in what appears to be an expression of disgust.

J Newborns can also discriminate among odours. They will turn their heads toward a sweet smell,
55 and their heart rate and respiration will slow down, indicating attention. Noxious odours, such as ammonia or rotten eggs, cause them to turn their heads away; heart rate and respiration accelerate, indicating distress. Infants
60 are even able to discriminate subtle differences in smells. After nursing for only a few days, an infant will consistently turn its head toward a pad saturated with its mother's milk in preference to one saturated with another
65 mother's milk (Russell, 1976). Only breast-fed babies show this ability to recognize the mother's odour (Cernoch & Porter, 1985). When bottle-fed babies are given a choice between their familiar formula and the smell
70 of a lactating breast, they will choose the latter (Porter *et al.*, 1992). Thus, there seems to be an innate preference for the odour of breast milk. In general, the ability to distinguish among smells has a clear adaptive value:
75 it helps infants avoid noxious substances, thereby increasing their likelihood of survival.

Source: Atkinson, R.L., Atkinson, R.C., Smith, E.E., Bem, D.J. & Nolen-Hoeksema, S. (1999).
***Hilgard's Introduction to Psychology,* (13ᵗʰ ed). Fort Worth: Harcourt Brace College Publishers.**

ENVIRONMENT **TODAY**

ACID RAIN IN NORWAY

Although some of the effects of acidic deposits from the atmosphere – so-called 'acid rain' – were identified nearly 5 150 years ago, the problem was only recognized as an international issue in the 1960s. This was when researchers in Scandinavia suggested that 10 much of the enhanced acidity precipitation falling there was due to the long-range transport of pollutants from other countries. Transboundary transport of pollution is now a widely accepted idea, and a number of international efforts to combat the problem have been launched. *Environment* 20 *Today* in this issue looks at the situation in Norway, where the acidification of freshwater ecosystems has shown some improvement in recent years.

25 Damage to rivers and lakes

Sulphur dioxide (SO_2) and nitrogen oxides (NO and NO_2, collectively referred to as NO_x)
have deleterious effects on many 30 parts of the environment on which they are deposited. They have adverse effects on human health, and on the growth of green plants, in which they 35 inhibit photosynthesis. Acid rain also damages buildings, corroding paint and metals and accelerating the weathering of some building stones. In 40 Norway the cost of this type of damage to buildings is estimated to be NOK 200–300 million (£16–24 million) each year.

The effects of acid rain on 45 soil and water depend upon their natural 'buffering capacity' – the ability of soil and water to neutralise incoming acids. This buffering capacity is 50 largely determined by the nature of the bedrock: ecosystems on hard, impervious igneous or metamorphic rock, with low calcium and magne- 55 sium contents, are most at risk of acidification from acid rain. All environments can withstand acid input up to a certain
level – the 'critical load', but 60 beyond that level significant changes occur.

Perhaps the most notable acid rain damage in Norway has been to freshwater ecosys- 65 tems. The death of fish is one of the most reliable indicators of acidification. Fish die for two main reasons. When acidification reaches a certain level, 70 young fish fresh from the spawn cannot survive. Different species have different levels of tolerance, but the most sensitive are trout 75 and salmon. The presence of aluminium is another common cause of fish death. Aluminium ions are washed out of soils and rocks by incoming hydrogen 80 ions in acid rain, and aluminium is toxic to fish because it prevents them from absorbing salts and destroys their gills.

One study of 1,679 lakes in 85 the south of the country in the 1970s found that brown trout were absent or had only sparse populations in more than half

Figure 1: Lime used to reduce acidification damage in Norway

Figure 2: Emissions of sulphur dioxide in Norway

Figure 3: Emissions of nitrogen oxides in Norway

the lakes. The proportion of lakes with no fish at all increased with declining pH levels (i.e., increasing levels of acidity). From 1960 to 1990, areas in southern Norway where fish stocks have been damaged have increased fivefold.

Combating acid rain damage

These depressing statistics of acid rain damage in Norway, largely concentrated in southern parts of the country, have generated action on a number of fronts. One method used to deal with the problem of acidified waters in the short term is the application of lime, to increase pH and reduce acid levels. In Norway, the use of lime has increased rapidly since the early 1980s, and in the mid-1990s about 120,000 tonnes were applied (Figure 1). In 1995, lime was applied in more than 2,500 locations, covering a precipitation area of about 6,400 km^2. However, lime can only repair acidification damage to a certain degree. It will never be a permanent solution.

In the long term, reduction of acid rain damage can only be achieved by reducing emissions of acid rain compounds at their source. To achieve these aims, a number of international agreements have been reached and, under these agreements, Norway has made three main political pledges:

- *to reduce sulphur dioxide emissions to 76% of the 1980 level;*
- *to stabilize oxides of nitrogen emissions at the 1987 level;*
- *to reduce oxides of nitrogen emissions to 70% of the 1986 level.*

On the sulphur dioxide front, Norway has almost achieved its aim already (Figure 2). Between 1980 and 1995, sulphur dioxide emissions were reduced by 75%

Table 1: Excess deposits of sulpher in Norway

Year	Area where critical load exceeded (% national land area)
1985	30%
1995	25%
2010	16%

due to increased taxes on sulphur in oils and a reduction in the sulphur content of light heating oils and diesel. Efforts to reduce emissions of nitrogen oxides have not been so successful (Figure 3). After an increase in emissions of 29% from 1980 to 1987, they were reduced by 5% in the period 1987–1995, and Norway remains one of the highest emitters of nitrogen oxides in Europe when measured in per capita terms. The goal of reducing emissions to 70% of the 1986 level seems unlikely to be achieved.

However, important though the efforts in Norway are, the fact remains that most of the acid rain falling on the country is emitted by other countries. No less than 95% of the sulphur deposited on Norway, and 86% of the nitrogen compounds, is due to long-range transboundary air pollution. Emissions from Great Britain and Germany, for example, each contribute more pollution to the Norwegian environment than domestic sources. Emissions from these and other countries are, however, also being reduced. The sulphur content of precipitation falling on Norway has fallen by more than 40% since 1980, and the goals set for countries by the Sulphur Protocol of 1994 aim to reduce it still further.

The 1994 Sulphur Protocol was a milestone in international pollution control in that it was based on the critical loads approach and assigned different levels of reduction to different countries, aiming to bring about environmental improvements at the lowest possible cost. Britain, for example, has committed to an 80% reduction in emissions by the year 2010 from the baseline year of 1980, while Germany's commitment is 87%. Most countries reached their reduction targets by the year 2000, but for some the full reductions will not be reached before 2010. The benefits of these reductions for Norway are already being felt. While 30% of Norwegian territory received amounts of sulphur that exceeded the critical load in 1985, this figure has been reduced by 25% by 1990 and should be cut to 16% by 2010 (Table 1).

Although there is no doubt that the acid rain problem in Norway, and elsewhere in Europe, is being tackled, one lesson of this is clear: preventing acid rain damage and rehabilitating affected ecosystems is a long-term exercise. For some acidified lakes, researchers believe that it might take more than 100 years before fresh waters regain something close to their original species composition with stable and maintained functions.

References

- Mason, C.F. (1996), *Biology of Freshwater Pollution*, 3rd edn, Longman.
- Morecroft, M. (1995), 'Air pollution and the nitrogen cycle,' *Geography Review*, Vol. 9, No 2, pp. 7–10.
- Whyatt, D. and Metcalf, S. (1995), 'Sulphur emissions and acid rain,' *Geography Review*, Vol. 9, No 1, pp. 14–18.

by NICK MIDDLETON

Nick Middleton *is a Lecturer in Physical Geography at St. Anne's and Oriel Colleges, Oxford University. His special interests include drylands and environmental issues.*

Source: Middleton, N., 1998. 'Acid Rain in Norway' in *Geography Review*, Vol. 11, No. 4., 6–7.

Text 3a-2: Skylarks in decline

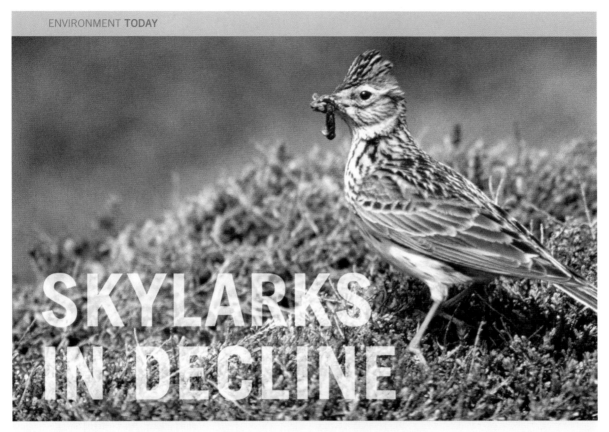

ENVIRONMENT **TODAY**

SKYLARKS IN DECLINE

The skylark is one of Britain's commonest birds, yet its population on farmland may have fallen by nearly 60% in just over 20 years. If we are to stop this decline, and hopefully reverse it, we need to understand the underlying causes, and to study the ecology of the species.

Where do we get our facts from? Britain and Ireland can be divided into 3,862 10km x 10km squares, and data on bird distribution are held by the British Trust for Ornithology (BTO), an organization concerned primarily with long-term surveys, population work and ringing and migration studies. From time to time, distribution records of different groups are published. When *The Atlas of Breeding Birds in Britain and Ireland* was published in 1976 it revealed that the skylark was the most widespread bird in Britain

and Ireland – present in 98% of the 10km squares. Skylarks were known to breed in 86% of the squares in which they were recorded and probably bred in the other 14%.

The total skylark population in Britain and Ireland in 1976 was estimated to be between two and four million pairs, on the assumption that each 10km square would hold between 500 and 1,000 breeding pairs. However, this involved some degree of informed guesswork because skylarks live in such a wide variety of open habitats with low vegetation (mainly grasslands, but also heaths, moors, salt marshes and farmland) and relatively little was known about population densities outside farmland.

During 1988–1991 there was a repeat scheme published as *The New Atlas of Breeding Birds in Britain and Ireland.*

When the number of 10km squares occupied was compared with those occupied in 1968–72, it revealed that skylarks had lost a small amount of ground – about 3%. The new scheme's more detailed work on the numbers of birds produced a more reliable estimate for the skylark population, concluding that there were about two million pairs in Britain and a further 570,000 in Ireland. It might seem that the estimate of 2.57 million pairs fits within the earlier estimate, but when we look at the part of the survey for which we have most detail, a different story emerges.

Decline on lowland farms

The only detailed evidence we have of any decline concerns skylarks on lowland farmland. We have no firm evidence for other habitats, and it is most

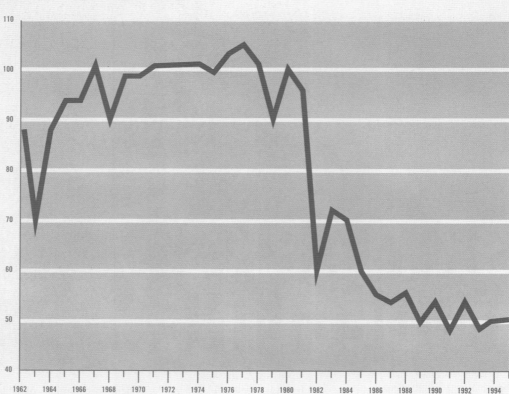

Figure 1: *Common Bird Census* indices for Skylark, 1962–1994

important to remember this when discussing falling skylark numbers. We know that on lowland farmland (which the *New Atlas* shows as having the highest densities of breeding skylarks) the breeding population has fallen by about 58% over a 20-year period (see Figure 1). This huge decline has been mirrored in other common farmland birds, including grey partridge, turtle dove, barn owl and corn bunting. The source of our evidence is the BTO's long-running *Common Birds Census*. Repeated annually, the census uses a mapping technique to produce a year-by-year index for all the species involved, calculated against a 'reference' or 'datum' year (1980) where the index is given an arbitrary value of 100. The indices provide a handy way of plotting the population ups and downs of a large number of species and, importantly, of identifying longer-term trends.

Possible reasons for the decline

It is clear that something has gone badly wrong for farmland birds during the last 20–25 years. To find out what has happened to the skylark, and why, and also to investigate means of putting the situation right, the Royal Society for the Protection of Birds has begun a new research programme. It is likely that what we learn about skylarks will have some relevance to other farmland species too.

Most of us only see skylarks singing high in the sky. They build a simple grass-lined nest among grass or crops, and chicks and adults feed on seeds, leaves, worms, insects and larvae. There have been radical changes in agri-cultural practices over the last 25 years and, given what is already known about skylark ecology, it is reasonable to infer that these changes are implicated in its decline.

(1) Increased areas of cereals
It seems likely that the widespread change from mixed farming regimes to monoculture has had a profound effect on skylarks. The disappearance of grass meadows may have meant a reduction in insect food available for chicks, for instance. Where a variety of crops were grown, skylarks could always find suitable nest-sites, and since cropping patterns and timing varied so much they could enjoy a prolonged breeding season. Cereal monocultures, on the other hand, provide much less choice and are also only suitable for nesting for a very short period.

Text 3a-2: Skylarks in decline cont.

A skylark nest in a Suffolk wheatfield

Skylark feeding her young

A skylark's nightmare! Cereal crops are aiding the decline

160 This timing problem has probably been made worse by the modern practice of autumn sowing – the crops become too dense for nest-sites very early in the season. Autumn sowing has also led to the virtual dis-

165 appearance of winter stubbles, which we know were very important sources of skylark food in winter. Skylarks would almost certainly fare much

170 better with more spring sowing, or at least a mixture of this and autumn sowing.

(2) Reduction of insect food by pesticides

175 Autumn sowing and the monoculture system depend on heavy applications of pesticides. A combination of insecticides and herbicides probably reduces insect

180 food supplies both for adult and young skylarks, and destroys many insect food plants. In addition, because pesticides are applied very early in the growth

185 cycle with autumn-sown cereals, it is very likely that insect food is greatly reduced by spring, when young skylarks need it most.

(2) Reduction of insect food in intensively managed pastures

190 Intensively managed pastures, with high densities of grazing livestock and heavy applications of nitrogen fertilizer to maxi-

195 mize the production of good grass, are bad news for skylarks, and this is not just because more animals means a greater chance

200 of nests being trampled. The dense, uniform sward produced is not very good for nesting and carries far fewer insects than old-fashioned pastureland.

Designing a plan of action

205 We know already that skylarks fare better on mixed farmland, and also where organic farming is practised. They do very well, too, on 'set-aside land', which is either

210 land put out of crop production for several years, or fields or field margins from which no crop is taken for a year. Farmers are compensated for setting land aside, and it can

215 help to reduce some persistent weeds. We have a number of ideas about how the situation could be improved for skylarks elsewhere, but we need to translate ideas and

220 intuition into a programme supported by good science. For this reason, the RSPB has embarked upon a three-year research programme, investigating skylark

225 ecology on 12 farms in three counties – four each in Norfolk, Oxfordshire and Dorset. This gives a good regional spread to the work, but it also involves three dif-

230 ferent categories of farm on predominantly arable land where cattle and sheep are reared, and in mixed farming areas.

If we are to begin to help sky-

235 larks, we must find out a great deal more about precisely what they need from a modern farming landscape. The research will tell us which habitats they feed in, both

240 in summer and in winter; exactly what adults and chicks eat; how breeding success varies on different crop types, and whether this varies from farm to farm and

245 between regions; and, hopefully, more about winter survival. In three years' time we hope that our action plan for skylark conservation will be much improved by

250 this new research input.

Further reading

- RSPB (1996) 'Crisis point,' Birds, the magazine of the RSPB, Vol. 16, Issue 3, pp 17–21.
- RSPB (1996), 'The Skylark', Birds, the magazine of the RSPB, Vol. 16, Issue 3, pp 24–27.

by MIKE EVERETT

Mike Everett *works for the Royal Society for the Protection of Birds (RSPB), Europe's largest voluntary wildlife conservation organization, with one million members. The RSPB's primary function is to conserve the UK's birds and their habitats, both through the promotion of more wildlife-friendly planning and land-use policies. The Society is increasingly involved with similar work overseas and is the UK partner of the global conservation body Birdlife International. Detailed investigation of the ecology of declining and Red List bird species is an important aspect of the Society's applied research.*

Source: Everett, M. (1997). Skylarks in decline. *Biological Sciences Review*, 10(2), 7-10.

The Economist, June 7th, 2008

Telemedicine comes home

Telemedicine permits remote consultations by video link and even remote surgery, but its future may lie closer to home.

Few places on earth are as isolated as Tristan da Cunha. This small huddle of volcanic islands, with a population of just 269, sits in the middle of the South Atlantic, 1,750 miles from South Africa and 2,088 miles from South America, making it the most remote settlement in the world. So it is a bad place to fall ill with an unusual disease, or suffer a serious injury. Because the islands do not have an airstrip, there is no way to evacuate a patient for emergency medical treatment, says Carel Van der Merwe, the settlement's only doctor. 'The only physical contact with the outside world is a six- to seven-day ocean voyage,' he says. 'So whatever needs to be done, needs to be done here.'

Nevertheless, the islanders have access to some of the most advanced medical facilities in the world, thanks to Project Tristan, an elaborate experiment in telemedicine. This field, which combines telecommunications and medicine, is changing as technology improves. To start with, it sought to help doctors and medical staff exchange information, for example by sending X-rays in electronic form to a specialist. That sort of thing is becoming increasingly common. 'What we are starting to see now is a patient–doctor model,' says Richard Bakalar, chief medical officer at IBM, a computer giant that is one of the companies in Project Tristan.

A satellite-internet connection to a 24-hour emergency medical centre in America enables Dr Van der Merwe to send digitised X-rays, electrocardiograms (ECGs) and lung-function tests to experts. He can consult specialists over a video link when he needs to. The system even enables cardiologists to test and reprogram pacemakers or implanted defibrillators from the other

Text 3b: Telemedicine comes home cont.

Telemedicine comes home

side of the globe. In short, when a patient in Tristan da Cunha enters Dr Van der Merwe's surgery, he may as well be stepping into the University of Pittsburgh medical centre. It is a great comfort to local residents, says Dr Van der Merwe, knowing that specialist consultations are available.

Most of the technology this requires is readily available, and it was surprisingly simple to set up, says Paul Grundy, a health-care expert at IBM. The biggest difficulty, he says, was to install the satellite-internet link. In theory, this sort of long-distance telemedicine could go much further. In 2001 a surgeon in New York performed a gall-bladder removal on a patient in Paris using a robotic-surgery system called Da Vinci. Although that was technologically impressive, it may not be where the field is heading.

Home is where the technology is

For advances in telemedicine are less to do with the *tele-* than with the *medi-cine*. In the long term, it may be less about providing long-distance care to people who are unwell, and more about monitoring people using wearable or implanted sensors in an effort to spot diseases at an early stage. The emphasis will shift from acute to chronic conditions, and from treatment to prevention. Today's stress on making medical treatment available to people in remote settings is just one way telemedicine can be used–and it is merely the tip of a very large iceberg that is floating closer and closer to home.

That is because telemedicine holds great promise within mainstream health care. Countless trials are under way to assess technology that can monitor people who have been diagnosed with heart conditions, or diseases like diabetes, from the comfort of their own homes. Rather than having their devices periodically checked at a clinic, some pacemaker patients can now have their implants inspected via mobile phone. That way, they need only visit the clinic when it is absolutely necessary.

Similarly, BodyTel, based in Germany, is one of several firms to have developed sensors based on Bluetooth wireless technology that can measure glucose levels, blood pressure and weight, and upload the data to a secure web server. Patients can then manage and monitor their conditions, even as they give updates to their doctors. Honeywell, an American industrial giant, has devised a system that patients can use at home to measure peak flow from their lungs, ECG, oxygen saturation and blood pressure, in order to monitor conditions ranging from lung disease to congestive heart failure. Doctors continually review the data and can act, by changing the patients' medication, for example, if they spot any problems.

This sort of thing appeals to both patients and health-care providers alike. The patients keep their independence and get to stay at home, and it costs less to treat them. And as populations age in developed countries, the prospect of being able to save money by treating people at home looks increasingly attractive.

It is not just people with diagnosed conditions who are starting to receive this kind of equipment. Since 2006, Britain has spent £80m ($160m) on 'preventative technology grants', which provide special equipment to enable 160,000 elderly people to stay in their homes.

Most of today's technology, however, calls on the patients to remember to monitor themselves, and also requires them to operate the equipment. For some patients, such as those in the early stages of Alzheimer's disease, that is impractical. So a lot of work is being done to automate the monitoring process and make the equipment easier to use.

William Kaiser and his colleagues at the University of California, Los Angeles, have developed a 'smart cane' to help monitor and advise people convalescing at home, for example. 'It has force sensors that measure pressure at the tip of the cane and around the handle. It also has motion sensors and accelerometers,' says Dr Kaiser. It uses these to calculate the gait of the patient and work out how they are doing with the cane, giving them feedback about how they could make better use of it to recover from, for example, a hip replacement. 'It provides guidance, either as beeps or it can talk to you,' he says.

The Economist, June 7th, 2008

225 Another approach is to use sensors embedded in the home. Oliver Goh of Implenia, a Swiss building-management firm, has come 230 up with a system to monitor the well-being of the occupant of a house. Using sensors on doors and mattresses, smart pill boxes that can tell 235 when they are being opened, heart-monitors and a location-sensing wristwatch–the system allows carers to keep tabs on elderly people. Implenia now 240 has six elderly volunteers lined up to test the technology, says Mr Goh. He hopes that if they have a heart attack, cannot get out of bed 245 or need help, their carers will soon know. Ultimately, he says, the aim is to see if this sort of approach can help to extend life expectancy.

250 **Prevention is better than cure**
Looking even further ahead, some day it may make sense to give these technologies to 255 healthy people, the 'walking well'. If sensors can monitor people without a threat to their privacy or comfort, doctors may be able to spot 260 diseases before the patient notices any symptoms. 'It's moving from telemedicine to telehealth and teleprevention,' says Dr Grundy of 265 IBM. It could also improve the efficiency of health-care systems, he says.

This kind of approach could save money as well as 270 spotting illnesses early, says Dr Kaiser. 'We'll detect them earlier when the cost of treatment and impact on an individual will be less,' he says. 275 The technology for this does not yet exist, admits John Linkous, executive director of the American Telemedicine Association. 'There still isn't a 280 device that can give you a complete body check,' he says. 'But I'm very optimistic about it in the long run.'

One idea is to use wire-285 less infra-red skin sensors to measure blood-count, heart-rhythm and the level of oxygen in the blood. Another is to implant wireless sensors 290 powered by the wearer's own body heat. Yet another common idea is to use smart toilets that can monitor human waste for the telltale 295 signs of intestinal disease or cancer. The hard part is not so much developing the sensor technology, says Dr Linkous, as sifting through the 300 results. 'It would produce a tsunami of data, and the problem is that we aren't set up with health-care systems that can deal with all that,' he says.

305 The answer will be even more technology, says Dr Bakalar. 'There has to be a way of filtering this information so that it doesn't over-310 whelm the medical services,' he says. The obvious approach is to use 'expert systems' – software programmed with expert med-315 ical knowledge and that can make clinical judgments.

Like telemedicine, expert systems have been around for some time. Trials in 320 Denmark, to advise doctors how to prescribe, suggest the technology has great scope. Sometimes they can reach better clinical judgments than 325 human experts do. But they are not widely used, partly because doctors are unwilling to be bossed around by a computer in the corner, but 330 also because they have been difficult to integrate into medical practice. They could be ideally suited to telehealth, however, quietly sifting 335 through the data generated by sensors and only raising the alarm and calling in their human colleagues when it becomes necessary to do so.

340 The shift from telemedicine to telehealth reflects a broader shift from diagnosis and treatment to 'wellness'. Taken to its technological 345 conclusion, this would involve using wireless sensors and implants to screen entire populations for early signs of disease as they go about their 350 daily lives. If it can be made to work, the days of making an appointment to see your doctor when you are not feeling well could be over. 355 Instead, it may well be your doctor who calls you.

Source: Telemedicine comes home. (2008, 7 June) [Electronic version]. *Economist* 387(8583), 28-30.

STATISTICS

◆◆◆

WITHOUT TEARS

SECTION 1

MAKING SENSE OF EXPERIENCE

It is by making sense of our experience that we human beings grow wiser and gain greater control over the environment we live in. This has been true for the development of the human race over the centuries. It is equally true for each of us as individuals in our own lifetimes. Fortunately, we
5 have this capacity for noticing things. We observe people, things and events in the world around us. We notice their similarities and differences, their patterns and regularities – especially when such features could endanger us or, alternatively, be turned to our advantage.

Many of our observations involve us in counting and
10 measuring. Perhaps we do so in rough-and-ready fashion, and often so intuitively that we are scarcely aware of this habit of 'quantification'. Nevertheless our observations and comparisons are often in terms of 'how much?', 'how big?', 'how often?', 'how far?', 'how difficult?', 'how quickly?', 'how well?', and so on.

15 Sometimes our observations concern a single thing or person or event. For example, we may notice the size of the potato crop in a particular field this year. We may make several observations about the same thing: not only the size of the crop in this field but also how much fertilizer was used, the nature of the soil, how much sunshine and rain it
20 had, etc. Sometimes our observations concern several similar but different things. For example, we may observe the size of the potato crop in several different fields this year, or in the same field over a succession of years.

Thus, we may make one or more observations on one individual, or we may do so for several individuals. Soon we have a
25 *collection* of observations (or 'data', to use the technical jargon).

Inquisitively, as if by instinct, we start looking at connections and patterns, similarities and differences, among the things we happen to have noticed. We ask ourselves questions about the data.

For example, what questions might we ask in looking for connections
30 among the data we have collected about the size of potato crops?

STATISTICS WITHOUT TEARS – MAKING SENSE OF EXPERIENCE

SECTION 2

We might ask: is the size of the crop similar in all fields this year? Or, is it similar in this field from one year to another? If not, why not? What else is different about those fields, or years, that might explain the differences?

35 All such questions lead to an even more vital one: what can we learn from the connections we see among this collection of data that might help us act more effectively in the future?

This is where statistics comes in. It has been developed as a way of making sense of collections of observations. It aims, particularly,
40 to help us avoid jumping to conclusions and to be cautious about the extent to which we can *generalize* from our always limited experience.

The tendency to generalize is an essential part of our everyday thinking. Because this particular field was generously treated with a
45 certain fertilizer and gave a bigger than usual potato crop, we may feel inclined to generalize and suggest that, therefore, *other* fields so treated would give bigger than usual potato crops.

Would you think it safe to generalize in this way – on the basis of experience with one field? Why, or why not?

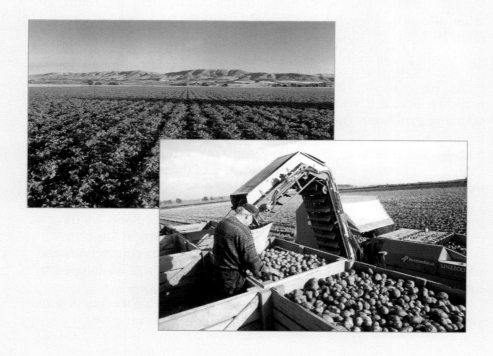

STATISTICS WITHOUT TEARS – MAKING SENSE OF EXPERIENCE

SECTION 3

50 In fact, such a generalization would be rather dangerous – it is very likely to be wrong. The bigger crop may be due not to the fertilizer but to, say, the weather. (That is, we may have jumped to an incorrect conclusion.) So even the same field, treated in the same way with fertilizer, may give a very different yield in another year.

55 And as for the other fields, they may differ in yet other ways that could influence the potato yield, e.g., type of soil, crop grown in the previous year, prevalence of plant disease in neighbouring fields, and so on. (Hence the weakness in our generalization.)

So, what is true of one field in one year may not be true of the 60 same field in other years, let alone of other fields. If we want to generalize more confidently, we need more experience – more observations. The more fields we look at, and over more and more years, the more confident we can be in suggesting how the potato crop is likely to turn out in other, similar fields.

65 But notice the word 'likely' in the sentence above. 'Likelihood' or 'weighing up the chances' (that is, 'probability') is central to the statistical view of the world. It recognizes no 100% certainties, especially when dealing with individual people, things or events. For example, a particular kind of field may, *in general*, produce a bigger 70 potato crop if treated in a certain way, but there will be many exceptions.

In which of these two cases would you think me more likely to be proved correct:

(a) If I predict that fields of a certain type will, in general, 75 produce a bigger crop if treated in such-and-such a way? or

(b) If I predict that any such *particular* field you care to pick out will do so?

STATISTICS WITHOUT TEARS – MAKING SENSE OF EXPERIENCE

SECTION 4

I'd be more likely to be correct in (a) than in (b). While such fields in general (maybe nine out of ten of them) will behave as expected, I
80 can't be sure that any one particular field you happen to choose will be one of those that do.

As you will learn, statistics helps us to look for reliable regularities and associations among things 'in general' and 'in the long run'. At the same time, however, it teaches us proper caution in
85 expecting these to hold true of any particular individuals. The two chief concerns of statistics are with (1) summarizing our experience so that we and other people can understand its essential features, and (2) using the summary to make estimates or predictions about what is likely to be the case in other (perhaps future) situations.

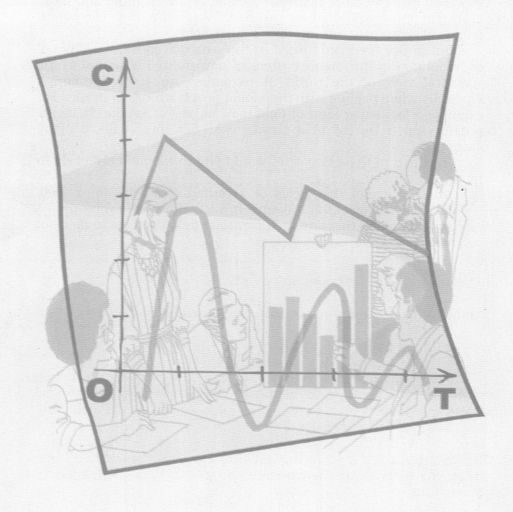

Text 4-2: What is statistics?

SECTION 5

WHAT IS STATISTICS?

90 Before we go any further, we'd better take note, in passing, that the word 'statistics' is used in at least four different senses. First of all, it can indicate, very broadly, a whole *subject* or *discipline*, and everything that gets studied or practised in its name. Secondly, and more specifically, the term may refer to the *methods* used to collect or

95 process or interpret quantitative data. Thirdly, the term may be applied to *collections of data* gathered by those methods. And fourthly, it may refer to certain *specially calculated figures* (e.g., an average) that somehow characterize such a collection of data. Thus, to illustrate the four meanings in turn, a researcher in a firm's

100 *statistics* department may use *statistics* (statistical methods) to gather and interpret *statistics* (data) about the revenue from sales of a new detergent, and may summarize his findings by quoting the *statistics* of 'average sales per thousand of population' in various towns and 'range of sales revenue from town to town'.

105 The meaning I shall emphasize in this book is the second of those mentioned above: statistics as a set of *methods of inquiry*. It is these methods that enable us to think statistically – a very powerful way to think – about a variety of situations that involve measurements or observations of quantities.

110 Few professional activities are untouched by statistical thinking, and most academic disciplines use it to a greater or lesser degree. Its applications in science, especially the 'biological sciences' like genetics, medicine and psychology, are both numerous and well known. But the physical sciences (e.g., meteorology, engineering and

115 physics) also need statistical methods. And even in the humanities, the dating of ancient fragments of textile or pottery has been revolutionized by the essentially statistical technique of radio-carbon dating; while statistical methods have also been used in literary studies to help decide such questions as whether a particular author

120 wrote a certain work, or at what point in his lifetime it was written. Statistics has developed out of an aspect of our everyday thinking to become a ubiquitous tool of systematic research.

But it is time we got down to discussing what it is about statistical thinking that can lend itself to such a variety of pursuits.

125 Statistics arises out of caution in the face of uncertainty. Statistical thinking is a way of recognizing that our observations of the world can never be totally accurate; they are always somewhat uncertain. For instance, a child we record as being four feet in height will not be exactly that – somewhere between 3 feet $11\frac{1}{2}$ inches and 4 feet $\frac{1}{2}$

STATISTICS WITHOUT TEARS – WHAT IS STATISTICS?

130 inch maybe, but not exactly four feet. And the chance of inaccuracy is even greater if we use our present observations to estimate what observations elsewhere might reveal. Thus, we might want to use our knowledge that four feet is the average height in this child's class to predict the average height in another class.

135 In such matters there can be no certainty. But statistics enables us to estimate the extent of our errors. Thus, we may express near certainty that the child's height lies within a range of four feet plus or minus half an inch; or we may calculate that the chances are ninety-nine in a hundred that the average height in another class lies 140 within two inches of four feet.

Text 4-3: Descriptive and inferential statistics

STATISTICS WITHOUT TEARS – DESCRIPTIVE AND INFERENTIAL STATISTICS

DESCRIPTIVE AND INFERENTIAL STATISTICS

You will find that statistics textbooks commonly make a distinction between (1) 'descriptive statistics' (methods used to summarize or describe our observations), and (2) 'inferential statistics' (using those observations as a basis for making estimates or predictions, i.e., inferences about a situation that has not yet been observed).

Look again at those three 'everyday' statements I mentioned earlier. Which of them appear(s) 'descriptive' and which 'inferential', in the sense indicated above?

(i) 'On average, I cycle about 100 miles a week';

(ii) 'We can expect a lot of rain at this time of year';

(iii) 'The earlier you start revising, the better you are likely to do in the exam'.

STATISTICS WITHOUT TEARS – DESCRIPTIVE AND INFERENTIAL STATISTICS

SECTION 7

Statement (i) is descriptive (an attempt to summarize experience), while (ii) and (iii) go beyond what is likely to happen in
155 the future.

The distinction between descriptive and inferential statistics depends upon another: the distinction between *samples* and *populations*.

In statistical jargon, 'population' does not necessarily refer to a
160 body of people. It may refer to people, but it may equally well refer to white mice, to light bulbs of a particular brand, to substandard dwellings in inner Birmingham, to meteorites, to future examination results in British secondary schools, and so on. The point is that population refers to *all* the cases or situations that the 'statistician'
165 wants his inferences or guesses or estimates to apply to. Thus, different statisticians may be making inferences about the learning ability of (all) white mice; predicting how long all light bulbs of a particular type are likely to burn; estimating the cost of renovating (all) substandard dwellings; predicting the composition of (all)
170 meteorites; guessing the (total) numbers of candidates passing various examinations, and so on.

Perhaps it is also worth pointing out that the researcher will not be interested in every aspect of members of a population. Rather, he is interested in just some – maybe only one – of the many attributes
175 or characteristics that members might have in common. Thus a psychologist may not be concerned to speculate about the tail-length or litter-size of white mice (though these characteristics might interest other researchers); he is interested simply in their learning ability. Neither might the astrophysicist be interested in predicting
180 the geographical distribution or the size of falling meteorites as well as their composition.

However, even if he is interested in only one characteristic of his population, the researcher will be most likely to study all members of it. Usually he has to do the best he can with a SAMPLE – a relatively small
185 selection – from within the population. Often he must do this to save time and expense. For the astrophysicist to tour the world inspecting every meteorite that has ever been known to fall would be prohibitively expensive. Again, an industrial researcher who is estimating the burning-life of a brand of light bulb by 'testing to
190 destruction' cannot test all the population or there will be none left to sell.

In some cases, it may be logically impossible to study all members of the population. The population may be infinite, or simply not yet available for study. Thus, the psychologist who is studying learning
195 ability in white mice will hope his results, and therefore his inferences,

STATISTICS WITHOUT TEARS – DESCRIPTIVE AND INFERENTIAL STATISTICS

will have some application to all white mice – not just the millions that exist at this moment but also the further millions not yet born. He may even hope his results can be generalized to explain *human* learning. Likewise, the astrophysicist may well use his statistics to generalize not
200 just about the meteorites that have already fallen to earth, or even about those that will fall in future; he may hope to speculate also about the composition of other objects flying around in space.

All such researchers go *beyond* the available information. They generalize from a sample to a population, from the seen to the
205 unseen. (So do we all, though often in a rather careless, uncontrolled way, when using everyday 'common sense'.) This idea of generalizing from a sample applies to research in the arts as well as in the sciences. For example, one would not have to have read everything ever written by, say, D.H. Lawrence and Joseph Conrad before one could
210 begin generalizing about how they compared and contrasted as novelists. One could work from a sample of two or three books by each author.

Anyway, *descriptive* statistics is concerned with summarizing or describing a sample. *Inferential* statistics is concerned with generalizing
215 from a sample, to make estimates and inferences about a wider population. Consider a biologist experimenting with the feeding of chicks. He may report (using descriptive statistics) that particular samples of 60 chicks, fed a particular compound, grow faster than a similar sample fed on some standard diet. So much (the weight gain) he
220 reports as fact. But he goes beyond fact. He uses inferential statistics to suggest that *all* similar chicks (the wider population) would grow faster if given similar treatment.

How safe are such generalizations from a part to a whole? Well, that is largely what statistics is about: quantifying the probability of
225 error. We will be looking at the underlying ideas in subsequent chapters. One thing we can say at this stage, however: the reliability of the generalization will depend on how well the sample mirrors the population – in other words: is the sample truly representative of the population?

Source: Rowntree, D. (1982). *Statistics without tears: a primer for non-mathematicians.* Harmondsworth: Penguin.

COMMON QUESTIONS ABOUT
CLIMATE CHANGE
• United Nations Environment Programme •
• World Meteorological Organization •

The scientists listed below have volunteered their time to write and review this brochure. The brochure is co-sponsored by the United Nations Environment Programme and the World Meteorological Organization. In addition, the United Nations Environment Programme, the National Oceanic and Atmospheric Administration, the U.S. Global Change Research Program and the Rockefeller Brothers Fund contributed funds for the layout and printing of the brochure. Leonie Haimson and Christine Ennis assisted in editing and Elizabeth C. Johnston and Julianne Snider designed the layout of the brochure.

AUTHORS
- Steven R. Hamburg
  Brown University, USA
- Neil Harris
  European Ozone Research Coordinating Unit, UK
- Jill Jaeger
  International Institute for Applied Systems Analysis, Austria
- Thomas R. Karl
  National Oceanic and Atmospheric Administration, USA
- Mack McFarland
  *United Nations Environment Programme
  (on loan from the DuPont Company), Kenya*
- John R. B. Mitchell
  Hadley Centre for Climate Prediction & Research, UK
- Michael Oppenheimer
  Environmental Defense Fund, USA
- Benjamin D. Santer
  Lawrence Livermore National Laboratory, USA
- Stephen Schneider
  Stanford University, USA
- Kevin E. Trenberth
  National Center for Atmospheric Research, USA
- Tom M.L. Wigley
  National Center for Atmospheric Research, USA

REVIEWERS/CONTRIBUTORS
- Daniel L. Albritton
  National Oceanic and Atmospheric Administration, USA
- Bert Bolin
  Chairman of the Intergovernmental Panel on Climate Change, Sweden
- Theresa Cookro
  National Oceanic and Atmospheric Administration, USA
- Susana B. Diaz
  Ozone and UV Laboratory, CADIC/CONICET, Argentina

- Robert E. Dickinson
  University of Arizona, USA
- Christine A. Ennis
  National Oceanic and Atmospheric Administration, USA
- Paul J. Fraser
  Commonwealth Scientific and Industrial Research Organization, Australia
- Hartmut Grassl
  World Meteorological Organization, Switzerland
- Ann Henderson-Sellers
  Royal Melbourne Institute of Technology, Australia
- John Houghton
  Co-Chair, Intergovernmental Panel on Climate Change Working Group II, UK
- Phil Jones
  University of East Anglia, UK
- Igor L. Karol
  Main Geophysical Observatory, Russia
- Murari Lal
  Indian Institute of Technology, India
- Jerry D. Mahlman
  National Oceanic and Atmospheric Administration, USA
- Pim Martens
  University of Limburg, The Netherlands
- Mario J. Molina
  Massachusetts Institute of Technology, USA
- Henning Rodhe
  University of Stockholm, Sweden
- Keith P. Shine
  University of Reading, UK
- Peter E.O. Usher
  United Nations Environment Programme, Kenya

This document answers some of the most commonly asked questions about the impact of human activity on climate change.
www.gcrio.org/ipcc/qa/contributors.html

Text 5-2: Common questions about climate change

COMMON QUESTIONS
ABOUT CLIMATE CHANGE

A   This document answers some of the most commonly asked questions about climate change, including whether the Earth has warmed, which human activities are contributing to climate change, what further climatic changes are expected to occur, and what effects these changes may have on humans and the environment.

5 <u>First, however, several issues have to be clarified: what the Earth's climate is, how climate differs from weather, and what processes influence climate.</u>

B   Climate is the average weather, including seasonal extremes and variations, either locally, regionally, or across the globe. In any one location, weather can change very rapidly from day to day and from year to year, even within an unchanging climate.

10 These changes involve shifts in, for example, temperatures, precipitation, winds, and clouds. In contrast to weather, climate is generally influenced by slow changes in features like the ocean, the land, the orbit of the Earth about the sun, and the energy output of the sun.

C   Fundamentally, climate is controlled by the long-term balance of energy of the

15 Earth and its atmosphere. Incoming radiation from the sun, mainly in the form of visible light, is absorbed at the Earth's surface and in the atmosphere above. On average, absorbed radiation is balanced by the amount of energy returned to space in the form of infrared 'heat' radiation. Greenhouse gases such as water vapour and carbon dioxide, as well as clouds and small particles (called 'aerosols'), trap some

20 heat in the lower part of the Earth's atmosphere. This is called the greenhouse effect. If there was no natural greenhouse effect, the average surface temperature would be about 34°C (61°F) colder than it is today.

D   Winds and ocean currents redistribute heat over the surface of the Earth. The evaporation of surface water and its subsequent condensation and precipitation in

25 the atmosphere redistribute heat between the Earth's surface and the atmosphere, and between different parts of the atmosphere.

E   Natural events cause changes in climate. For example, large volcanic eruptions put tiny particles in the atmosphere that block sunlight, resulting in a surface cooling of a few years' duration. Variations in ocean currents change distribution of heat and

30 precipitation. El Niño events (periodic warming of the central and eastern tropical Pacific Ocean) typically last one to two years and change weather patterns around the world, causing heavy rains in some places and droughts in others. Over longer time spans, tens or hundreds of thousands of years, natural changes in the geographical distribution of energy received from the sun and the amounts of greenhouse gases and

35 dust in the atmosphere have caused the climate to shift from ice ages to relatively warmer periods, such as the one we are currently experiencing.

F   Human activities can also change the climate. The atmospheric amounts of many greenhouse gases are increasing, especially that of carbon dioxide, which has increased by 30% over the last 200 years, primarily as a result of changes in land use

40 (e.g., deforestation) and of burning coal, oil, and natural gas (e.g., in automobiles, industry, and electricity generation). If current trends in emissions were to continue, the amount of carbon dioxide in the atmosphere would double during the 21st century,

with further increases thereafter. The amounts of several other greenhouse gases would increase substantially as well.

G 45   The accumulation of greenhouse gases in the atmosphere due to human activities will change the climate by enhancing the natural greenhouse effect, leading to an increase in the Earth's average surface temperature. This warming may be partially offset in certain regions where air pollution leads to high concentrations of small particles in the atmosphere that block sunlight.

H 50   The current best estimate of the expected rise of globally averaged surface temperature relative to 1991 is 1 to 3.5°C (about 2 to 6°F) by the year 2100, with continued increases thereafter. Because most greenhouse gases remain in the atmosphere for a long period of time, even if emissions from human activities were to stop immediately, effects of past emissions would persist for centuries.

I 55   The Intergovernmental Panel on Climate Change (IPCC), co-sponsored by the United Nations Environment Programme and the World Meteorological Organization and made up of over 2,000 scientific and technical experts from around the world, published its First Assessment Report in 1990 and its Second Assessment Report in 1996. The Second Report contains over 10,000 references and is over 2,000 pages in 60 length. Although our understanding of some details of climate change is still evolving, the IPCC report is the most comprehensive and scientifically authoritative account of our understanding of climate change, the potential impact on humans and the natural environment, the technology currently available to reduce human influences on climate, and the socio-economic implications of possible measures to mitigate these 65 changes. The document that follows has been written and reviewed by scientists who participated in the IPCC process, and it attempts to answer some of the most commonly asked questions about these issues, based upon information contained in the IPCC reports. A list of the scientists who prepared this document is provided inside the front cover.

Figure 1.1

Schematic view of components of the global climate system, some of their processes and interactions, and some aspects that can cause climate change.

Text 5-3: Are human activities contributing to climate change?

ARE HUMAN ACTIVITIES
CONTRIBUTING TO CLIMATE CHANGE?

A A comprehensive assessment by the IPCC of the scientific evidence suggests that human activities are contributing to climate change, and that there has been a discernible human influence on global climate.

B Climate changes caused by human activities, most importantly the burning of
5 fossil fuels (coal, oil, and natural gas) and deforestation, are superimposed on, and to some extent masked by, natural climate fluctuations. Natural changes in climate result from interactions such as those between the atmosphere and ocean, referred to as internal factors, and from external causes, such as variations in the sun's energy output and in the amount of material injected into the upper atmosphere by
10 explosive volcanic eruptions.

C Studies that aim to identify human influences on climate attempt to separate a human-caused climate-change factor (the signal) from the background noise of natural climate variability. Such investigations usually consist of two parts: detection of an unusual change, and attribution of all or part of that change to a particular cause or causes.

D 15 The concepts of detection and attribution may be understood in terms of a simple medical analogy. Measurement of a body temperature of 40°C (104°F) detects the presence of some abnormal condition or symptom, but does not in itself give the cause of the symptom. To attribute the symptom to an underlying cause often requires additional and more complex tests, such as chemical analyzes
20 of blood and urine, or even X-rays and CAT scans.

E Early work on climate change detection examined changes in the globally-averaged surface temperature of the Earth over the last century. Most studies of this type concluded that the observed increase of roughly 0.5°C (about 1°F) was larger than would be expected as a result of natural climate variability alone.

F 25 Observed globally-averaged temperature changes have also been analyzed away from the Earth's surface. The observations used come from conventional weather observing instruments (radiosondes) and from satellites. As expected, because of the different factors affecting the variability of and persistence of temperatures at different altitudes, there are noticeable differences between short-term trends at
30 the surface and those at higher altitudes. The record of temperatures away from the Earth's surface, which spans only the past 40 years compared with the much longer surface record, is too short for globally-averaged values to provide any definitive information about the extent of human influences.

G The further step of attributing some part of observed temperature changes to
35 human influences makes use of climate models, which have been employed to estimate the climatic effects of a range of human-induced and natural factors. The human factors include recent changes in the atmospheric concentrations of both greenhouse gases and sulphate particles (called 'aerosols'). The natural factors include solar variability, the effects of volcanic eruptions, and internal variability of the climate system resulting
40 from interactions among its individual components.

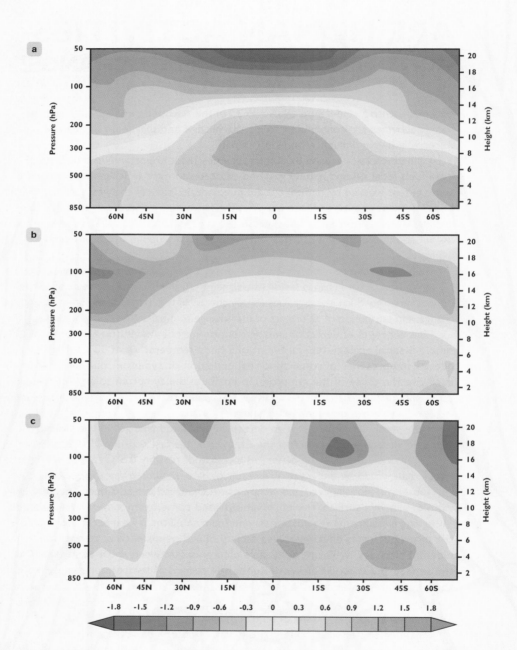

Figure 2.1

Modelled and observed changes in atmospheric temperature, from close to the Earth's surface to the lower stratosphere. Model results are from two sets of experiments: with 'present-day' levels of atmospheric carbon dioxide (panel a), and with present-day carbon dioxide, sulphur emissions, and stratospheric ozone depletion (panel b). They are given as changes relative to a pre-industrial state of the atmosphere. Observed changes (panel c) are temperature trends over the period 1963 to 1988, as estimated from weather balloons. All results are for annually averaged data and are in units of degrees Celsius (panels a, b) and degrees Celsius/25 years (panel c). The patterns of change in panels b and c are similar.

Text 5-3: Are human activities contributing to climate change? cont.

H   The changes in globally averaged temperature that have occurred at the Earth's surface over the past century are similar in size and timing to those predicted by models that take into account the combined influences of human factors and solar variability.

I   To probe the question of attribution requires the application of more powerful
45 and complex methods, beyond the use of global averages alone. New studies have focused on comparing maps or patterns of temperature change in observations and in models. Pattern analysis is the climatological equivalent of the more comprehensive tests in the medical analogy mentioned previously, and makes it possible to achieve more definitive attribution of observed climate changes to a
50 particular cause or causes.

J   The expected influence of human activities is thought to be much more complex than uniform warming over the entire surface of the Earth and over the whole seasonal cycle. Patterns of change over space and time therefore provide a more powerful analysis technique. The basic idea underlying pattern-based approaches is
55 that different potential causes of climate change have different characteristic patterns of climate response or fingerprints. Attribution studies seek to obtain a fingerprint match between the patterns of climate change predicted by models and those actually observed.

K   Comparisons between observed patterns of temperature change and those
60 predicted by models have now been made at the Earth's surface and in vertical sections through the atmosphere (Figure 2.1). Model predictions show increasing agreement with changes observed over the past 30–50 years. The closest agreement occurs when the combined effects of greenhouse gases and sulphate aerosol particles are considered. Statistical analyses have shown that these correspondences are highly
65 unlikely to have occurred by chance.

L   The agreements between the patterns of change predicted by models and those actually observed are due to similarities at large spatial scales, such as contrasts between the temperature changes in the northern and southern hemispheres or between different levels of the atmosphere. It is at these large scales that we have
70 most confidence in model performance. More importantly, many of the results of these studies agree with our physical understanding of the climate system, and do not depend solely on numerical models or statistical techniques.

M   There are still uncertainties in these detection and attribution studies. These are due primarily to our imperfect knowledge of the true climate-change signal
75 due to human activities, to our incomplete understanding of the background noise of natural climatic variability against which this signal must be detected, and to inadequacies in the observational record. Such uncertainties make it difficult to determine the exact size of the human contribution to climate change. Nevertheless, the most recent assessment of the science suggests that human
80 activities have led to a discernible influence on global climate and that these activities will have an increasing influence on future climate.

WHAT HUMAN ACTIVITIES
CONTRIBUTE TO CLIMATE CHANGE

The burning of coal, oil, and natural gas, as well as deforestation and various agricultural and industrial practices, are altering the composition of the atmosphere and contributing to climate change. These human activities have led to increased atmospheric concentrations of a number of greenhouse gases, including carbon
5 dioxide, methane, nitrous oxide, chlorofluorocarbons, and ozone in the lower atmosphere. The importance of these gases is shown in Figure 3.1.

Carbon dioxide is produced when coal, oil, and natural gas (fossil fuels) are burned to produce energy used for transportation, manufacturing, heating, cooling, electricity generation, and other applications (see Figure 3.2). The use of fossil fuel currently
10 accounts for 80 to 85% of the carbon dioxide being added to the atmosphere.

Land use changes, e.g., clearing land for logging, ranching, and agriculture, also lead to carbon dioxide emissions. Vegetation contains carbon that is released as carbon dioxide when the vegetation decays or burns. Normally, lost vegetation would be replaced by regrowth with little or no net emission of carbon dioxide. However,
15 over the past several hundred years, deforestation and other land use changes in many countries have contributed substantially to atmospheric carbon dioxide increases. Although deforestation is still occurring in some parts of the northern hemisphere, on the whole, regrowth of vegetation in the north appears to be taking some carbon dioxide out of the atmosphere. Most of the net carbon dioxide
20 emissions from deforestation are currently occurring in tropical regions. Land use changes are responsible for 15 to 20% of current carbon dioxide emissions.

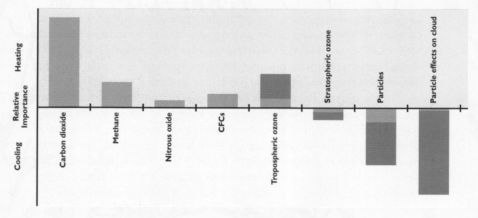

Figure 3.1
Relative importance of the various greenhouse gases and small particles currently in the atmosphere. Bars extending above the horizontal line indicate a warming effect. Bars extending below the horizontal line indicate a cooling effect. The impacts of tropospheric ozone, stratospheric ozone, and particles are quite uncertain. The range of possible effects for these gases is indicated by the bar on the darker shading; i.e., the effect is in the range of one end of the darker shading to the other.

Text 5-4: What human activities contribute to climate change cont.

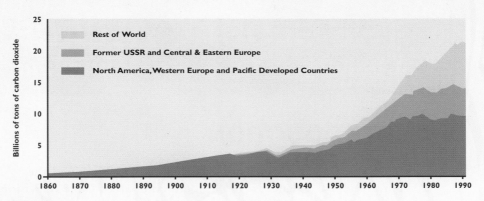

Figure 3.2

Carbon dioxide emissions from the burning of coal, oil, and natural gas are shown for the period 1860 to 1995 for three groups of countries.

Methane (natural gas) is the second most important of the greenhouse gases resulting from human activities. It is produced by rice cultivation, cattle and sheep ranching, and by decaying material in landfills. Methane is emitted during coal mining and oil drilling, and by leaky gas pipelines. Human activities have increased the concentration of methane in the atmosphere by about 145% above what would be present naturally.

Nitrous oxide is produced by various agricultural and industrial practices. Human activities have increased the concentration of nitrous oxide in the atmosphere by about 15% above what would be present naturally.

Chlorofluorocarbons (CFCs) have been used in refrigeration, air conditioning, and as solvents. However, the production of these gases is being eliminated under existing international agreements because they deplete the stratospheric ozone layer. Other fluorocarbons that are also greenhouse gases are being used as substitutes for CFCs in some applications, for example in refrigeration and air conditioning. Although currently very small, their contributions to climate change are expected to rise.

Ozone in the troposphere, that is, in the lower part of the atmosphere, is another important greenhouse gas resulting from industrial activities. It is created naturally and also by reactions in the atmosphere involving gases resulting from human activities, including nitrogen oxides from motor vehicles and power plants. Based on current data, tropospheric ozone is an important contributor to the enhanced greenhouse effect. However, in part because ozone is also produced naturally, and because of its relatively short atmospheric lifetime, the magnitude of this contribution is uncertain.

Contrary to popular perception, the Antarctic ozone hole does not cause global warming. Instead, the global depletion of stratospheric ozone caused by CFCs and other gases has resulted in a small cooling effect as shown in Figure 3.1.

Human activities, such as the burning of fossil fuels and changes in land use, have increased the abundance of small particles in the atmosphere. These particles can change the amount of energy that is absorbed and reflected by the atmosphere. They are also believed to modify the properties of clouds, changing the amount of energy that they absorb and reflect. Intensive studies of the climatic effects of these particles began only recently and the overall effect is uncertain. It is likely that the net effect of these small particles is to cool the climate and to partially offset the warming of increasing concentrations of greenhouse gases.

Source: United Nations Environment Programme – World Meteorological Organization (1997, last modified May 24, 2006). *Common questions about climate change.* Retrieved January 15, 2009, from the U.S. Global Change Research Information Office website: http://www.gcrio.org/ipcc/qa/index.htm

THE GLOBAL VILLAGE:
Challenges for a shrinking planet

INTRODUCTION

Since the Canadian academic Marshall McLuhan coined the phrase 'global village' in 1969, home computers, cable television, satellite-linked mobile phones and the Internet have been added to the array of new technologies drawing the peoples of the world
5 together. But McLuhan also pointed out that the tribal-global village is not 'the place to find ideal peace and harmony'. Village conditions bring into focus the myriad differences between people and cultures.

Multinationals seeking to exploit the potential of economic
10 globalization are often advised to 'think global, act local'. While the idea of a single global purchasing culture may appeal to big business, the reality is that people's buying habits are determined as much by culture as by income – and cultures vary greatly from place to place. What sells well in Japan may stay on the shelves in
15 Canada. While some products appear to have global appeal, selling methods and local specifications may vary considerably. Even in the European Union, where trading and political ties are especially strong, there are major differences in customer behaviour. Advertising which works for Italians may turn off Scandinavians.
20 The German consumer products market is different from that in neighbouring France. This multiplicity in buying patterns extends to many other aspects of daily life – politics, food, hobbies, education and sexual relations. Even with a single country, diversity is often more apparent than homogeneity. Lager louts
25 who like to create mayhem in the streets of Paris may share a plane home with culture vultures on an art appreciation tour. Every city is a mishmash of humanity of all shades, habits and opinions. On a global scale, this variety is almost infinite.

It is sometimes argued that developments in transport and
30 telecommunications, along with the collapse of communism, have resulted in the 'deaths' of distance, geography and history. In other words, people share the same view of the world whichever continent they inhabit. They are joined together by a desire to enjoy freedom, material comfort, and security. Television and the Internet
35 have created new links between people worldwide. Sport, fashion and entertainment have become global industries. Political

cooperation between nations, especially in Europe but also in intergovernmental forums in Latin America, East Asia and Africa, is much greater than it was before World War II. For all its
40 weaknesses, the UN system provides an extraordinary concentration of intergovernmental debate and cooperation. The growth of trade, tourism and foreign investment strengthens the bonds between countries and should make them less likely to fight each other. Conversely, any country which gets left out of the global system or
45 feels threatened by it, may be tempted to lash out. Hence concerns over, for example, North Korea or Iraq.

In terms of economic management, the World Bank model (based on western thinking) is used almost everywhere. Yet opinions differ strongly on the effectiveness of 'structural adjustment
50 programmes' and the mix of private/public control over economic activity. The Asian financial crisis may throw up more resistance to the idea of aping the US model of society, flawed by urban deprivation and violent crime. The 'global village' is perhaps closest in the financial world, where London, Tokyo, New York and about
55 20 other cities dominate a 24-hour global trading system for stocks, bonds, currencies, commodities and financial derivatives. In this screen-based village, vast sums are transferred back and forth in deals which are mostly speculative rather than directly connected to trade in merchandise or services. This 'virtual' economy can have a huge
60 impact on real lives in every part of the world. The power and global reach of the money men causes unease among both peoples and governments. While poorer countries feel exposed to economic domination by the West, the growing business habit of 'outsourcing' (i.e., exporting jobs) creates new tensions in richer nations, where
65 public concern over the environment has also increased. The World Trade Organisation (WTO) regulates trade but does not address the social or ecological consequences of global business activity – a shortcoming which many feel must be urgently addressed.

The disengagement of the global financial system from the real
70 economy is a worrying development, especially in the light of potential penetration by organized crime. The problem with this and other aspects of globalization is that there are no effective global authorities to control it. Nations are very reluctant to share sovereignty with other countries, so the move towards effective
75 supranational institutions is slow. The US, which did so much to create the UN system in the 1940s, has become increasingly laggard in this respect. Unfortunately, the global village lacks an effective police force.

THE SHRINKING PLANET

Telecommunications and transportation systems have weakened the barriers of geography which separate different peoples. Yet many cultural differences persist.

Global communications – global understanding?

5 In 1995, according to the International Telecommunication Union (ITU), there were 211 TV sets for every 1,000 people in the world. Even in sub-Saharan Africa there were 43 sets per thousand people. Few cultural groups are so isolated that they 10 don't know how their fellow humans live. But this knowledge can increase discontent as well as cultural convergence. According to *Time* magazine, the 1998 football World Cup accumulated a total TV audience of 37 billion people – more than six times the global population. 15 Brazil's young star Ronaldo became one of the best-known people in the world. Similar fame has been accorded to media 'stars' as diverse as President Clinton, Arnold Schwarzenegger and the Pope.

For most of human history, the picture of the world which most people had was determined by their immediate surroundings. There was no way of 20 knowing what was happening on the other side of the planet – other than from the stories and artefacts brought back by a few sailors, explorers or merchants.

The 20th century has seen a profound change. Not only has the population exploded (from 2 billion in 1930 to about 6 billion now), but technology has enabled tribesmen in Central Africa or Borneo to watch TV programmes 25 about life in New York or Paris; throngs of tourists visit the most remote corners of the globe, bringing with them new ideas, customs and languages; aboriginal groups have learned to use the Internet to publicise their grievances at the encroachment of alien modern cultures which threaten tribal traditions; books written in Germany or Canada are routinely printed in Spain or Hong 30 Kong; components of motor cars designed in Japan may be made in a dozen different countries before being assembled in Mexico or Poland; people in Korea or Tanzania may share admiration for Manchester United, Michael Jackson, Ronaldo or Princess Diana; wearing jeans, eating burgers and listening to rock music have become the daily habit of youngsters across the globe.

35 Yet such apparently universal links may be more superficial than they seem. An Iranian youth cannot easily shake off the Islamic culture in which he grew up. While Shanghai teenagers may appear to have more in common with their counterparts in Los Angeles than with the older generation in other oriental cities, they remain distinctly Chinese, affected by their national culture, history and 40 language. Just as it is possible for an individual to be a 'good European' as well as a proud Scotsman, so fellow citizens of the 'global village' can share many tastes and yet be as different from each other as chalk from cheese.

Sharing common interests and buying similar products do not obliterate human peculiarities. Indeed, the homogenising effect of globalization is partly

45 offset by computer technology which allows for easy customisation of products.
A 'world car' may have the same 'platform', but is sold with different shapes,
colours and accessories to meet local requirements. Ownership of global media
is highly concentrated, but communication is being fragmented as digital
technology enables hundreds of TV channels to be beamed to different
50 audiences with their own viewing tastes and receiving languages.

ECONOMIC GLOBALIZATION

Money is increasingly stateless, with most countries abandoning exchange controls. Businesses of all sizes can now operate on a global basis.

The global marketplace

5 Money and goods are moved from country to country
with little regard for distances or borders. More and
more services are traded internationally. On the other
hand, labour remains largely immobile (and therefore
vulnerable to job losses) – an anomaly which can have
10 serious social implications. The growth in international
trade is a telling indicator of the globalization of
business in recent decades. Between 1900 and 1950,
world trade barely doubled. Since then, the volume
of trade has risen twelvefold. In OECD countries, the
15 majority of goods used by households and industries
include imported materials or parts. Complex
manufacturing activities now span the globe.

A Perhaps the most obvious sign of globalization is in the economic area. The
logos of corporate giants such as Coca-Cola, Nike, Shell and Mercedes are a
20 common sight in cities on every continent. While trade has long been a part
of the international scene, its volume has rocketed in the last decade, along
with foreign capital investment. Business operates in a worldwide environment,
with competition in faraway countries as much of a threat to a manufacturer
or service provider as a rival in a neighbouring town.

B 25 In 1996, foreign direct investment (FDI) around the world was $553 billion
– more than twice the figure for 1990 ($239 billion). The biggest recipient
countries were the US ($77 billion), China ($40 billion), the UK ($32 billion)
and France ($22 billion), followed by Brazil ($10 billion), Singapore ($9 billion),
Indonesia, the Netherlands and Mexico ($8 billion each), and Australia, Canada
30 and Spain ($6 billion each). Some $15 billion was invested in the former Soviet
bloc in Europe and Central Asia. Elsewhere in the developing world, Malaysia,
Peru, India, Argentina, Chile, Colombia, Thailand, Venezuela, Vietnam, the
Philippines and Nigeria all had FDI exceeding $1 billion. Meanwhile, global
merchandise exports grew from $1.9 trillion in 1980 to $5.4 trillion in 1996.

35 Trade in services has leapt ahead too. For example, it has become commonplace
    for European airlines to get their computer programming done in Asia and for
    banks, accountants and advertising agencies to sell their services in dozens of
    different countries.

(C)   Services and intellectual property rights are now covered by the
40 international rules of the World Trade Organization, making it easier and more
    lucrative for companies to sell services and know-how across borders. Trade in
    goods has been encouraged by the fall in tariff barriers brought about by
    successive GATT[1] rounds. The weighted mean tariff for products entering the
    European Union was down to 5% by 1997 and just over 4% in the US. The
45 comparative figure for Japan was less than 3%. India's weighted mean tariff fell
    from 83% in 1990 to 27.7% in 1997 as it gradually opened itself to
    international trade and investment.

(D)   Of course, tariffs do not tell the whole story, since trade can equally be
    impeded by cultural differences, domestic regulation, language barriers and, as
50 the World Bank delicately puts it, 'private collusive behaviour and information
    asymmetries'.

(E)   The three most powerful trading blocs are the EU, APEC and NAFTA,
    which together account for over 90% of international trade. Economic
    globalization is a phenomenon which impacts on all countries but which is of
55 main benefit to the industrialised world – which has goods to sell and money
    to buy. Africa, the 'lost continent', has increased its trade with the outside
    world but its share of global FDI and trade is tiny.

(F)   One of the dangers of economic globalization is the further concentration
    of power in those who are already rich. The gap between rich and poor
60 nations has widened in recent years, despite the catch-up success of a few
    countries such as the Asian 'tigers'. A similar division is taking place between
    individual haves and have-nots even within the industrialised countries. Those
    without money are pushed to the margins of society, while commercial
    thinking spreads from business to penetrate socio-cultural sectors such as
65 education, health care, the arts and even religion.

(G)   Globalization, as driven largely by short-term economic pressures, is based
    on consumerism, with people being regarded primarily as 'customers'. They are
    segmented by income group rather than by cultural differences. The value of, say,
    social manners or communal worship tends to be submerged, along with 'non-
70 economic' considerations such as animal rights or the 'health' of the oceans.

(H)   Yet the image of global business as a juggernaut destroying everything in
    its path is misleading. Companies may try to shape consumer demand but
    cannot disregard customer concerns such as health and environment. The more
    sophisticated companies take care to emphasize their social responsibilities,
75 working more closely with governments and NGOs to ensure that
    'sustainability' is built into their long-term business plans. For example,
    Unilever's support for the Marine Stewardship Council shows how economic
    power can be used to protect global resources.

1 After 1947, rules for international trade were negotiated by member states in the General Agreement on Tariffs
and Trade (GATT) – the US congress having rejected the idea of an international trade organization as part of the
original UN system. For over 40 years, the GATT remained a provisional set of international trading rules rather than
a regulatory authority as such. The last round of GATT negotiations, known as the Uruguay Round, was completed
in 1994. It greatly extended the range of trade covered and finally established the World Trade Organization, based
in Geneva, to act as a global regulatory authority.

Competition and protection

80 The pressures of global competition may tempt some countries to protect their own workers from job losses by increasing trade barriers. Advocates of free trade argue that such policies result in a vicious circle of retaliatory action – and point to the protectionist, war-provoking 1930s as a grim example.

85 *The increase in global trade means that exchange rate fluctuations now play a major role in determining business success or failure. Even the best-managed company can be destroyed by a sudden move in the exchange rates. For example, businesses in Japan had to contend with a fall in the exchange rate of the yen* 90 *from 111 to the US dollar in mid-1970 to 147 in August 1998. During the same period, the Indonesian rupiah fell from 2,500 to 14,000.*

The supermarket has replaced the corner shop as the symbol of household consumerism in the global village. In 95 the West, the contents of a typical house contain products from every corner of the globe. Supermarket shelves are stacked with food brought from dozens of countries. In a pre-industrial village, what was available was largely determined by what could be grown on surrounding farms. 100 No such limitations exist in the global village.

Global financial markets

Financial services in the global village are heavily concentrated in a few OECD countries. For example, the world's stock markets carried a market capitalisation value of $20,178 billion in 1997, with the US accounting for 42% of this vast sum. The 105 leading stock markets (measured by the capital value of all stocks listed in 1997) were:

	$ billion
US	8,484
Japan	3,089
UK	1,740
Germany	671
China (inc. HK)	656
France	591

Note that US stock market capitalisation grew from $3,059 billion in 1990, while Japan's total barely increased from its 1990 level. Market capitalisation of the Hong Kong exchange rose from $83 billion in 1990 to $450 billion in 1996, China's from $2 billion to $206 billion.

In mid-1998, the Frankfurt and London stock exchanges announced that they planned to 115 develop a joint electronic trading platform. Other European exchanges may decide to join later, raising the prospect of a single European stock exchange – though Paris initially reacted to the Anglo-German plan by proposing its own combination of exchanges. The large OECD countries dominate global banking, and trade in foreign exchange, commodity futures, stocks and shares, and financial 'derivatives'. Global derivatives contracts were valued at $55.5 trillion 120 in 1995. The combined weight of these money markets, whose activity (including daily turnover of $1.2 trillion in foreign exchange) is largely speculative – as opposed to being driven by merchandise trade ($5 trillion a year) – dwarfs global GNP ($27.8 trillion). This situation has led some commentators to describe the global financial system as 'casino capitalism' which has spun out of control and threatens the 'real economy'. Electronic funds transfers have greatly 125 increased the difficulty of controlling (and taxing) flows of money from country to country.

Whereas the World Trade Organization provides a global regulatory body for international trade in goods and services, there is no equivalent body for the regulation of global money markets.

COMMUNITY & CONFLICT

Citizens of the global village tend to be the better educated and more prosperous of the world's people. It is a new minority group, surrounded by the poor.

A   There is no inherent conflict between being a good global citizen and being a
5   proud member of a particular regional or ethnic group, nation state or city. The same person may regard himself as a 'European' or an 'African' while endorsing the universal brotherhood of man. Such multi-layering of identities is common. Humans long to be part of a group, while insisting on their individuality. The habit of treating a different tribe as the enemy may be accompanied by great
10   hospitality towards strangers. Awareness of the planet's fragility may have brought moves towards the globalization of human society, but the propensity to violent conflict seems as well-honed as ever. If global war now seems unlikely, civil wars still rage worldwide.

> ### Global village – global inequality
>
> 15   **There is little sign that the economic benefits of the global village will be evenly distributed. The income gap between rich and poor has widened over the last 50 years. The technology gap has yawned wider still.**

B   Ethnic divisions have not vanished but may gradually diminish under the influence of globalization. Coke and Pepsi show their customers as smiling multi-
20   ethnic crowds, implying that the world is already united in its love of soft drinks. Teenagers have their own global culture based on fashion, pop music, sports heroes and clothes. Sport is both unifying and polarising in its effect, with supporters cheering their own team and jeering their opponents.

C   More and more countries are becoming multi-ethnic, embracing large
25   numbers of foreigners. Though this creates tensions at first, the longer-term trend appears to be greater acceptance of multi-cultural society. Urbanization, another global phenomenon, has accelerated this trend, for it is easier to introduce new cultures in the relative anonymity of the city than it is in tradition-bound rural villages. In OECD countries almost 80% of the
30   population live in towns – compared to 31% in China and 27% in India. In global terms, the majority of people (54%) still live in rural areas. Yet rapid urbanization is a common feature of almost every developing country. New ideas and fashions – and diseases – spread fast in cities. In major urban centres of even the poorest countries there is a core of privileged people with access
35   to computers, mobile phones, electric razors, imported wines and other trappings of the global village.

D   A century ago agriculture employed over half the workforce even in rapidly industrializing countries. Today the global average is still over 45%. But in the UK and USA, farm workers now make up less than 3% of the workforce. Some
40   experts have suggested that a similar contraction is happening in manufacturing,

as technology enables more products to be made by computer–controlled
machines. Services already account for 70% of employment in the USA. Since
agriculture and manufacturing have provided the bulk of employment for
hundreds of years, the transition to a radically different pattern of employment is
45 bound to be difficult. Blaming the loss of jobs on globalization is a typical
reaction, with foreigners bearing the brunt of labour force discontent.

E   In 1995, Germany's population included over 7 million foreigners (compared
with the UK's 2 million). Germany received 788,000 immigrants in 1995. In
Australia, foreign-born workers make up 24% of the total labour force. The US
50 has about 25 million foreign-born residents, accounting for about 9% of the
workforce. There was a legal inflow of 721,000 in 1995 (compared with 1.5
million in 1990). Illegal immigrants probably number at least a million a year.
Foreigners make up 19% of the Swiss population and 9% of the population in
Austria and Belgium. The Middle East is home to large numbers of immigrant
55 workers from Egypt, Pakistan, Bangladesh and the Philippines. Workers from
Bolivia and Paraguay go to Argentina in search of a better life, just as Turks go to
Germany, Mexicans to the US and Algerians to France.

F   Whether the world is more prone to conflict than it used to be is hard to say.
Perhaps we are just more aware of violent confrontation in different parts of the
60 world. A famine in remote Sudan gets media coverage whereas a century ago
starving populations might die unseen. Today's wars can be watched live on
television, like Hollywood action movies. Greater awareness of the human
consequences of battle may reduce the lust for war – or make it another
spectator sport.

65 ### Fringe groups everywhere

70

The proliferation of nationalist militia groups in the
US – there are over 400 groups with paramilitary
training sites in over 20 states – is but one sign of
the fragmentation of modern society. Hundreds of
other fringe groups and 'eccentric' individuals have
been strengthened by the ability to link with others
through television and over the Internet. Thus
behaviour which was once regarded as bizarre
or anti-social, is increasingly regarded as a
75 'normal' part of the multi-cultural society.

G   Computer-mediated communication (CMC) is being used in more and
more countries as a way to enhance democracy. Over 200 cities worldwide
have civic networking projects experimenting in information access and
citizens' feedback and even voting. However, CMC is also used by less
80 desirable groups such as paedophile rings, gun salesmen, pornographers and
political extremists. For example, the Thule-Netz in Germany provides an
Internet-based information exchange which has different levels of access – to
ensure that only genuine right-wing activists know what is being planned. Use
of the World Wide Web gets round the problem of Germany's domestic ban on
85 the distribution of Nazi propaganda.

(H)   This example highlights a more general problem – how to enforce national law in the global village. Laws enacted to protect the people and environment of one country are increasingly undermined by new 'global' technology (e.g., electronic funds transfer) or by international agreements (e.g.,

90 greenhouse gas emissions) which tend to use a 'lowest common denominator' approach in order to get consent from as many nations as possible. Organized crime has been particularly adept at exploiting the weaknesses in global law enforcement, growing at a much faster rate than most legitimate businesses. Organized crime is a major beneficiary of the global village.

95 **Cultural diversity**

Cultural diversity is one of the glories of human civilization. For example, Chiapas Indians, using caricature blond wigs and pale-faced masks, adapted Spanish cultural imports to their own use after the invasion by Cortes in the 16th century. Similarly, Western cultural exports of the late 20th century (and early 21st century) are being

100 adapted in different ways in different parts of the world. Gunpowder and disease overthrew native societies in the colonial era. Television, mobile phones and soft drinks may do the same for traditional societies in the 21st century. A major complaint of today's Chiapas-based Zapatistas movement in Mexico is the damage done to native cultures by global capitalism and the exclusion of the masses from the

105 benefits which globalization is supposed to bring.

THE SHARING OF SOVEREIGNTY

There is more and more cooperation – and even pooled sovereignty – between states. Every country is strongly influenced by external factors beyond its control.

It is sometimes argued that globalization is breaking down the system of nation

5 states upon which international relations has largely depended. Just as families once combined into tribes and tribes into nations, so nations are combining into regional power blocs, and thence perhaps to a single world political community. Such an outcome is a very long way off, but there is certainly far more cooperation between nations than there was 50 years ago. Indeed, there is

10 now a vast network of international organizations, at both government and non–government levels, bringing people together to work on the practical issues of living together in harmony.

    While nation states remain the chief building blocks of the global system, they are by no means the only players on the scene. Chief among international

15 organizations is the United Nations – much maligned for its inability to solve the world's most intractable problems (civil war, poverty, etc.) yet an essential tool for the prevention of global anarchy. In fact, the UN has provided an invaluable

forum for the exchange of views and has provided the main coordinating centre
to deal with mundane but vital rules to ensure that international mail gets
20 delivered, that aircraft can fly across borders in safety, that food and industrial
goods meet specified health and safety standards. These daily achievements of UN
agencies go unreported, while failures of peace-making get much media
attention.

Bearing in mind the pressures on competing nations, it is perhaps
25 surprising that any major decisions can be made on a joint basis. That the
European Union was able to agree (in 1986) on a majority voting system to
advance the single market was an extraordinary development in international
relations. The EU has gone even further along this path with the agreement by
11 of its 15 member states to pursue economic and monetary union, including
30 the use of a single currency. In the EU, at least, national sovereignty over
economic matters has been pooled among 11 governments.

The United Nations

The United Nations organization
provides the nearest thing to a world
35 government. Though its impact is minimal
in resolving serious political conflicts,
the UN has many valuable functions in
smoothing international relations.

The UN is a kind of diplomatic
40 global village, which brings together
thousands of government officials
from 185 member countries. Their
primary aim is the preservation of
world peace – though UN work
45 extends to many other objectives. The
UN General Assembly, comprising
delegates from all UN member states,
is more representative of the world
community than the 15-nation Security
50 Council, but has far less power.
General Assembly resolutions, even
when passed with overwhelming
majorities, do not bind the Security
Council, which is dominated by the
55 'permanent five' – the US, China,
Russia, France and the UK.

Other bodies which tie Europe's nations closer together include the
European Free Trade Association, the Western European Union, the Council of
Europe and the Organization for Security and Cooperation in Europe. NATO
60 provides a military alliance which links the US and Canada with Europe, and
talks in the top-level 'Transatlantic Business Dialogue' envisage a free trade area
embracing both the European Union and North America.

International law

65 Most law is based on national legislation, but there is a steady accretion of international law. The UN has secured over 300 international treaties since 1945. Most countries have agreed to overriding global laws dealing with such matters as offshore territorial rights, marine pollution, international trade and nuclear 70 proliferation. EU directives take precedence over the national laws of 15 European countries.

Shared sovereignty

The European Union provides the world's most prominent example of shared 75 sovereignty. Since 1957, the EU has been engaged in an ambitious programme for 'ever closer union among the peoples of Europe'. Eleven of the 15 member states have agreed to a common economic and 80 monetary policy, including the use of a single currency, the euro. Though efforts to develop a common approach to foreign policy have so far failed, most of Western Europe has become a closely integrated 85 economic area, with strong political ties. The Social Chapter lays down broad principles for employee rights, while the EU has led the world in many areas of environmental law. The world's two other 90 main trading blocs, NAFTA and APEC, are not remotely like the EU in terms of political integration and have few of the EU's supranational rules on social and environmental protection.

95 Even the superpower US has relinquished some of its sovereignty by, for example, joining the World Trade Organization and agreeing to abide by its rules. It will be interesting to see how often the WTO's dispute settlement procedures are called into play over the next decade and whether major economic powers can be made to toe the line, even when it hurts their domestic business interests.
100 American support is vital if multinational institutions are to work. Yet the US opposed the 1997 Ottawa treaty on landmines and the mid-1998 UN decision to establish an International Criminal Court. Getting out of step with global opinion will damage US security options in the long run.

CONVERGING OR DIVERGING?

Tourism, transport and telecommunications have brought the world closer together, but new cultures are being created as fast as the old ones disappear.

Since 1945 there has been an underlying assumption that the world's poorer
5 countries are gradually 'developing' towards the western model and that
international aid policy should be geared to this end. The success of some
Asian countries, notably Japan (which was restructured under US guidance
after 1945), lent weight to this thesis. Though the World Bank now divides
countries into high, middle and low income countries, rather than developed
10 and developing countries, the basic premise has remained – countries afflicted
with high levels of poverty, disease and deprivation can improve their standards
by adopting western-style institutions and economic management.

    The governing elites of almost all states have come to accept that free markets,
combined with strict monetary discipline, offer the best path to improving living
15 standards. Country after country has adopted a World Bank-driven 'structural
adjustment programme' in an effort to achieve economic success. The orthodox
view is that public ownership and protected markets are less efficient than private
ownership and free trade. Governments around the globe, encouraged by the
World Bank, have been busy privatising state-owned companies in everything from
20 electricity generation and telecommunications to railways and even prisons. The
notion of 'public service', whether in health care or broadcasting, has given way to
'private enterprise'.

    Average living standards, life expectancy and educational norms have risen
strongly in dozens of countries since 1945, though the gap between rich and
25 poor countries is wider than ever. Very few 'developing' states have managed to
catch up on the wealthy 'establishment' in North America and Western Europe.
Most of the exceptions are in Asia, recently subject to financial meltdown.
'Development' has gone into reverse in Indonesia, and even Japan and South
Korea are suffering hardship. In other parts of the world, catching up has been
30 more dream than reality, at least for the vast bulk of the population. Latin
America, notorious for its uneven distribution of wealth, has had buoyant stock
markets, along with mass poverty. Living conditions in the former Soviet Union
have deteriorated for the majority while a few get very rich. Africa has scarcely
begun to improve the economic lot of its black population. If there is any
35 global pattern to all this, it seems to be that elites everywhere are doing very
well, while 'ordinary people' are facing insecurity and hardship – hardly a major
departure from historical precedent. Many people, in both the industrialised and
developing worlds, feel that globalization threatens their jobs, indeed their
whole way of life.

40   There seems to be no way to insulate a modern economy from the forces
of global capitalism, yet unease about the direction such forces are taking
humanity is by no means confined to Muslims worried about western 'moral
corruption', or Buddhists forsaking the material world. Islamist Iran has tried

The excluded society

45 Poverty and ignorance rule out full participation in the global high-tech economy for much of the world's population. Their exclusion could be a source of growing instability.

50 'Excluded' from the global consumer society by poverty, Peruvian children know as little about 'information technology' as they do about how their Inca ancestors were able, without the use of machinery, to

55 build walls from massive but perfectly-fitted stone blocks. Power over information and invention has always been confined to elites. Ownership of modern technology is heavily concentrated in a few OECD countries. Yet

60 computers have given ordinary citizens access to more information about technology and government than has ever been available before. Optimists argue that the result will be better education, more

65 opportunity and stronger democracy.

Cultural invasions

Tourist visits worldwide more than doubled between 1980 and 1996, reaching almost 600 million. Television

70 and branded products reach almost every part of the globe. But the way that local populations react to such 'cultural invasions' varies greatly.

Networked computers

75 dramatically increase the power of information exchange worldwide – for scientific purposes (accelerating invention), for social and political activism (gathering like-minded

80 individuals) and for business (identifying and selling into new markets). A key characteristic of the Internet is its chaotic diversity. With the advent of digital television, giving

85 viewers hundreds (possibly thousands) of channels to choose from, 'chaotic diversity' may soon overtake television too – though standardised products are more profitable and media

90 ownership is highly concentrated.

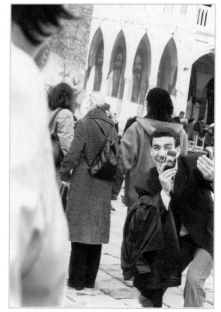

Text 6-6: Converging or diverging? cont.

to resist foreign influence, but the weakness of its economy has persuaded it to adopt a more open attitude. In recent years India has also turned away from self-sufficiency to more integration with the world economy. Even North Korea, facing severe food shortages and economic decline, is keen to attract 95 foreign investment.

Tourism has made the retention of traditional cultures more difficult while giving it new economic value – thus local festivals and tribal dances are mounted not as part of regional tradition but as a show for foreign visitors. The Czech Republic (population 10 million) had 17 million tourists in 1996. Most went to 100 Prague, transforming that city from the quiet shabbiness of the communist era to the bustling 'fast-food' commercialism of today. Such developments appear to reinforce the view that the world is being reshaped according to American values.

Of course, tourism is not just an American phenomenon. Germans, Britons, Japanese, Malaysians and many other nationalities travel abroad in very large 105 numbers. The total of overseas tourist visits was close to 600 million in 1996. Cheap air travel has made mass tourism possible, even to the most exotic places. The influx of tourists with different cultural values creates tensions in the receiving community – which may be suppressed when the economic benefit is sufficiently large but may rankle beneath the surface. Yet the local youths who 110 treat foreign visitors with a mixture of envy and contempt may well enjoy listening to rock music and smoking Marlboro cigarettes. They may dream of driving a BMW and having a mobile phone. Their families probably have a Japanese television set. In terms of 'brand allegiance', some global convergence has already taken place. Coca-Cola is an obvious example.

115 Global broadcasting has even greater impact on popular culture, as was shown by the extraordinary worldwide attention given to the death of Princess Diana (overshadowing the death of Mother Theresa). Watching global news coverage, TV soaps and sporting events is an experience shared by billions. Yet the advent of multi-channel broadcasting will enable viewers to customise their 120 viewing habits. In short, two trends are discernible – a global convergence of certain consumption patterns, combined with a vigorous interest in localised cultures – old and new. Diversity is still the main attribute of the global village.

Source: Buckley, R. (ed.). (1998). The Global Village: challenges for a shrinking planet. *Understanding Global Issues,* 98(7)

THE NEW LINGUISTIC ORDER

A As you read this sentence, you are one of approximately 1.6 billion people – nearly one-third of the world's population – who will use English in some form today. Although English is the mother tongue of only 380 million people, it is the language of the lion's share of the world's books, academic papers, newspapers,
5 and magazines. American radio, television, and blockbuster films export English-language pop culture worldwide. More than 80 per cent of the content posted on the Internet is in English, even though an estimated 44 per cent of online users speak another language at home. Not surprisingly, both the global supply of and the demand for English instruction are exploding. Whether we
10 consider English a 'killer language' or not, whether we regard its spread as benign globalization or linguistic imperialism, its expansive reach is undeniable and, for the time being, unstoppable. Never before in human history has one language been spoken (let alone semi-spoken) so widely and by so many.

B With unprecedented reach comes a form of unprecedented power. Although
15 language is synonymous with neither ideology nor national interest, English's role as the medium for everything from high-stakes diplomacy to air traffic control confers certain advantages on those who speak it. Predominantly English-speaking countries account for approximately 40 per cent of the world's gross domestic product. More and more companies worldwide are
20 making English competency a prerequisite for promotions or appointments. The success of politicians around the world also increasingly depends on their facility in English. When newly elected German chancellor Gerhard Schroeder and French president Jacques Chirac met in September to discuss future cooperation, they spoke neither French nor German, but English. And English
25 is the official language of the European Central Bank, despite the fact that the United Kingdom has not joined the European Monetary Union, the bank is located in Frankfurt, and only 10 per cent of the bank's staff are British. The predominance of English has become such a sore point within the European Union that its leadership now provides incentives for staff members to learn
30 any other official language.

C Yet professional linguists hesitate to predict far into the future the further globalization of English. Historically, languages have risen and fallen with the military, economic, cultural, or religious powers that supported them. Beyond the ebb and flow of history, there are other reasons to believe that the English
35 language will eventually wane in influence. For one, English actually reaches and is then utilized by only a small and atypically fortunate minority. Furthermore, the kinds of interactions identified with globalization, from trade to communications, have also encouraged regionalization and with it the spread of regional languages. Arabic, Chinese, Hindi, Spanish, and a handful of other
40 regional tongues already command a significant reach – and their major growth is still ahead. Finally, the spread of English and these regional languages collectively – not to mention the sweeping forces driving them – have created a squeeze effect on small communities, producing pockets of anxious localization and local-language revival resistant to global change.

LOVE THY NEIGHBOUR'S LANGUAGE

A map, post-World War I, showing the different languages spoken in different countries.

D English came to Massachusetts the same way it did to Mumbai: on a British ship. For all the talk of Microsoft and Disney, the vast reach of English owes its origins to centuries of successful colonization by England. Of the 100 colonies that achieved independence between 1940 and 1990, 56 were former British colonies and 1 was an American possession. Almost every colony that won its
50 independence from England either kept English as an official language or at least recognized its utility.

E The continued spread of English today is both a consequence of and a contributor to globalization. Some factors are obvious: the growth in international trade and multinational corporations; the ever-widening reach of
55 American mass media; the expanding electronic network created by the Internet; and the linguistic impact of American songs, dress, food, sports, and recreation. Other factors are perhaps less visible but no less powerful, such as the growth in the study of English overseas and the swelling number of students who go abroad to study in English-speaking countries. In 1992, almost half of the
60 world's million-plus population of foreign students were enrolled at institutions in six English mother-tongue countries: Australia, Canada, Ireland, New Zealand, the United Kingdom, and the United States.

52

F Yet globalization has done little to change the reality that, regardless of location, the spread of English is closely linked to social class, age, gender, and
65 profession. Just because a wide array of young people around the world may be able to sing along to a new Madonna song does not mean that they can hold a rudimentary conversation in English, or even understand what Madonna is saying. The brief formal educational contact that most learners have with English is too scant to produce lasting literacy, fluency, or even comprehension.
70 Indeed, for all the enthusiasm and vitriol generated by grand-scale globalization, it is the growth in regional interactions – trade, travel, the spread of religions, interethnic marriages – that touches the widest array of local populations. These interactions promote the spread of regional languages.

G Consider the case of Africa, where some 2,000 of the modern world's approximately
75 6,000 languages are spoken and 13 per cent of the world's population lives. English is neither the only nor even the best means to navigate this linguistic obstacle course. Throughout East Africa, Swahili is typically the first language that two strangers attempt upon meeting. The average East African encounters Swahili in a variety of contexts, from the market, elementary education, and government
80 'how to' publications, to popular radio programming and films. New movies from India are often dubbed in Swahili and shown in towns and villages throughout Kenya, Tanzania, and Uganda. In West Africa, some 25 million people speak Hausa natively and perhaps double that number speak it as a second or third language, due in large part to burgeoning regional business at local markets
85 throughout the region. Since most Hausa speakers are Muslim, many of them also attend Koranic schools where they learn Arabic, itself a major regional language in North Africa. Thus, many Africans are trilingual on a functional basis: local mother tongues among 'their own', Hausa for trade and secular literacy, and Arabic for prayer and Koranic study. Hausa speakers firmly believe that Hausa
90 has great prospects as a unifying language for even more of West Africa than it already reaches. Its main competition will not likely come from English but rather from other regional languages such as Woloff – which is also spreading in markets in and around Senegal – and Pidgin English.

H Increased regional communication, informal market interaction, and migration
95 are driving regional language spread around the world just as they are in Africa. Mandarin Chinese is spreading throughout China and in some of its southern neighbours. Spanish is spreading in the Americas. Hundreds of varieties of Pidgin English have emerged informally among diverse groups in Australia, the Caribbean, Papua New Guinea, and West Africa. The use of French is still
100 increasing in many former French colonies, albeit much more slowly than at its peak of colonial influence. Hindi is reaching new learners in multilingual, multiethnic India. And Arabic is spreading in North Africa and Southeast Asia both as the language of Islam and as an important language of regional trade.

I Some languages are spreading in part due to the efforts of organizations and
105 government committees. France spends billions of francs annually to support

53

French-language conferences, schools, and media that promote French as a vehicle for a common French culture. Muslim organizations in the Middle East spread knowledge about Islam worldwide with an extensive array of English pamphlets and other literature, but they cultivate their ties with each other in
110 Arabic. Moreover, in promoting Islam within their borders, many governments seek to Arabize local ethnic minorities (for example, Berbers in Morocco and Christians in Sudan). The German government funds 78 Goethe Institutes, scattered from Beirut to Jakarta, that offer regular German language courses as well as German plays, art exhibits, lectures, and film festivals. Singapore, a tiny
115 country with four official languages, is in the nineteenth year of its national "Speak Mandarin" campaign. Singapore designed the campaign to encourage dialect-speaking Chinese to adopt a common language and facilitate the use of Mandarin as a regional tongue.

J The importance of regional languages should increase in the near future. Popular
120 writers, itinerant merchants, bazaar marketers, literacy advocates, relief workers, filmmakers, and missionaries all tend to bank on regional lingua francas whenever there is an opportunity to reach larger, even if less affluent, populations. In many developing areas, regional languages facilitate agricultural, industrial, and commercial expansion across local cultural and governmental boundaries. They
125 also foster literacy and formal adult or even elementary education in highly multilingual areas. Wherever the local vernaculars are just too many to handle, regional languages come to the fore.

HOME IS WHERE THE TONGUE IS

K For all the pressures and rewards of regionalization and globalization, local identities remain the most ingrained. Even if the end result of globalization is to
130 make the world smaller, its scope seems to foster the need for more intimate local connections among many individuals. As Bernard Poignant, mayor of the town of Quimper in Brittany, told the *Washington Post*, 'Man is a fragile animal and he needs his close attachments. The more open the world becomes, the more ties there will be to one's roots and one's land.'

L In most communities, local languages such as Poignant's Breton serve a strong symbolic function as a clear mark of 'authenticity'. The sum total of a community's shared historical experience, authenticity reflects a perceived line from a culturally idealized past to the present, carried by the language and traditions associated (sometimes dubiously) with the community's origins. A concern for authenticity
140 leads most secular Israelis to champion Hebrew among themselves while also acquiring English and even Arabic. The same obsession with authenticity drives Hasidic Jews in Israel or the Diaspora to champion Yiddish while also learning Hebrew and English. In each case, authenticity amounts to a central core of

54

Text 7-1: The new linguistic order cont.

cultural beliefs and interpretations that are not only resistant to globalization but
145 are actually reinforced by the 'threat' that globalization seems to present to these
historical values. Scholars may argue that cultural identities change over time in
response to specific reward systems. But locals often resist such explanations and
defend authenticity and local mother tongues against the perceived threat of
globalization with near religious ardour.

M As a result, never before in history have there been as many standardized languages
as there are today: roughly 1,200. Many smaller languages, even those with far
fewer than one million speakers, have benefited from state-sponsored or voluntary
preservation movements. On the most informal level, communities in Alaska and
the American northwest have formed Internet discussion groups in an attempt to
155 pass on Native American languages to younger generations. In the Basque, Catalan,
and Galician regions of Spain, such movements are fiercely political and frequently
involve staunch resistance to the Spanish government over political and linguistic
rights. Projects have ranged from a campaign to print Spanish money in the four
official languages of the state to the creation of language immersion nursery and
160 primary schools. Zapatistas in Mexico are championing the revival of Mayan
languages in an equally political campaign for local autonomy.

N In addition to invoking the subjective importance of local roots, proponents of local
languages defend their continued use on pragmatic grounds. Local tongues foster
higher levels of school success, higher degrees of participation in local government,
165 more informed citizenship, and better knowledge of one's own culture, history, and
faith. Navajo children in Rough Rock, Arizona, who were schooled initially in
Navajo, were found to have higher reading competency in English than those who
were first schooled in English. Governments and relief agencies can also use local
languages to spread information about industrial and agricultural techniques as
170 well as modern health care to diverse audiences. Development workers in West
Africa, for example, have found that the best way to teach the vast number of
farmers with little or no formal education how to sow and rotate crops for higher
yields is in these local tongues. From Asturian to Zulu, the world's practical
reliance on local languages today is every bit as great as the identity roles these
175 languages fulfil. Nevertheless, both regionalization and globalization require that
more and more speakers and readers of local languages be multiliterate.

LOOKING AHEAD

O Since all larger language communities have opted to maintain their own
languages in the face of globalization, it should come as no surprise that many
smaller ones have pursued the same goal. If Germans can pursue globalization
180 and yet remain German-speaking among themselves, why should Telagus in
India not aspire to the same?

55

THE NEW LINGUISTIC ORDER

P Multilingualism allows a people this choice. Each language in a multilingual society has its own distinctive functions. The language characteristically used with intimate family and friends, the language generally used with co-workers or
185 neighbours, and the language used with one's bosses or government need not be one and the same. Reading advanced technical or economic material may require literacy in a different language than reading a local gossip column. As long as two or more languages are not rivals for the same societal function, a linguistic division of labour can be both amicable and long-standing. Few English speakers in India,
190 for example, have given up their local mother tongues or their regional languages. Similarly, in Puerto Rico and Mexico, English is typically 'a sometime tongue', even among those who have learned it for occupational or educational rewards.

Q There will of course be conflict, not to mention winners and losers. Language conflict occurs when there is competition between two languages for exclusive
195 use in the same power-related function – for example, government or schooling. Most frequently, this friction occurs when one regional or local language seeks to usurp roles traditionally associated with another local tongue. In the Soviet era, Moscow took an aggressive line on local languages, instituting Russian as the sole language of education and government in the Baltics and Central Asia. In the
200 1990s, however, many of these states had slowly deemphasized Russian in schools, government, and even theatres and publishing houses, in favour of their national tongues. Estonia, Latvia, and Lithuania passed the strictest laws, placing education, science, and culture within the exclusive purview of their national languages and (only just recently) leaving ethnic Russian out in the cold.

R Even though local and regional regimes are most likely to use language for political ends, global languages (including English, the language of globalization) can also foster conflict. France's anxiety over the spread of English is well documented. The government in Paris forbids English in advertising and regulates the number of English-language films that may be shown in the country. A cabinet-level official,
210 the minister of culture and communication, is responsible for monitoring the well-being of the national tongue. The Académie Française, France's national arbiter of language and style, approves official neologisms for Anglo-American slang to guard the French language against 'corruption'. Yet French schools are introducing students to English earlier and earlier.

S Those who speak and master the languages of globalization often suggest that 'upstart' local tongues pose a risk to world peace and prosperity. Throughout most of recorded history, strong languages have refused to share power with smaller ones and have accused them of making trouble – disturbing the peace and promoting ethnic violence and separatism. Purging Ireland of Gaelic in the nineteenth century,
220 however, did not convince many Irish of their bonds with England. Those who fear their own powerlessness and the demise of their beloved languages of authenticity have reasons to believe that most of the trouble comes from the opposite end of the language-and-power continuum. Small communities accuse these linguistic Big Brothers of imperialism, linguicide, genocide, and mind control.

56

T Globalization, regionalization, and localization are all happening concurrently. They are, however, at different strengths in different parts of the world at any given time. Each can become enmeshed in social, cultural, economic, and even political change. English is frequently the language of choice for Tamils in India who want to communicate with Hindi-speaking northerners. Ironically, for many
230 Tamils – who maintain frosty relations with the central authorities in Delhi – English seems less like a colonial language than does Hindi. In Indonesia, however, English may be associated with the military, the denial of civil rights, and the exploitation of workers, since the United States has long supported Jakarta's oligarchic regime. Although English is spreading among Indonesia's upper classes,
235 the government stresses the use of Indonesia's official language, Bahasa Indonesia, in all contact with the general public. Local languages are denied any symbolic recognition at all. The traditional leadership and the common population in Java, heirs to a classical literary tradition in Javanese, resent the favouritism shown to English and Indonesian. Spreading languages often come to be hated because they
240 can disadvantage many as they provide advantages for some.

U English itself is becoming regionalized informally and orally, particularly among young people, because most speakers today use it as a second or third language. As students of English are increasingly taught by instructors who have had little or no contact with native speakers, spoken English acquires strong regional
245 idiosyncrasies. At the same time, however, English is being globalized in the realms of business, government, entertainment, and education. However, Hindi and Urdu, Mandarin Chinese, Spanish and vernacular varieties of Arabic can all expect a boom in these areas in years to come – the result of both a population explosion in the communities that speak these tongues natively and the
250 inevitable migrations that follow such growth.

V The smallest languages on the world scene will be squeezed between their immediate regional neighbours on one side and English on the other. Most purely local languages (those with fewer than a million speakers) will be threatened with extinction during the next century. As a result, many smaller communities will
255 not only seek to foster their own tongues but also to limit the encroachments of more powerful surrounding languages. Even in a democratic setting, 'ethnolinguistic democracy' is rarely on the agenda. The US government was designed to protect the rights of individuals; it is no accident that its founding fathers chose not to declare an official language. Yet given the vocal opposition to Spanish-language
260 and bilingual education in many quarters of the United States, it seems not everyone holds the right to choose a language as fundamental.

W What is to become of English? It may well gravitate increasingly towards the higher social classes, as those of more modest status turn to regional languages for more modest gains. It might even help the future of English in the long run if
265 its proponents sought less local and regional supremacy and fewer exclusive functions in the United Nations and in the world at large. A bully is more likely to be feared than to be popular. Most non-native English speakers may come to

57

THE NEW LINGUISTIC ORDER

love the language far less in the 21st century than most native English speakers
seem to anticipate. Germans are alarmed that their scientists are publishing
270 overwhelmingly in English. And France remains highly resistant to English in
mass media, diplomacy, and technology. Even as English is widely learned, it
may become even more widely disliked. Resentment of both the predominance of
English and its tendency to spread along class lines could, in the long term,
prove a check against its further globalization.

X There is no reason to assume that English will always be necessary, as it is
today, for technology, higher education, and social mobility, particularly after its
regional rivals experience their own growth spurts. Civilization will not sink into
the sea if and when that happens. The decline of French from its peak of
influence has not irreparably harmed art, music, or diplomacy. The similar
280 decline of German has not harmed the exact sciences. Ancient Greek, Aramaic,
Latin, and Sanskrit – once world languages representing military might,
sophistication, commerce, and spirituality – are mere relics in the modern world.
The might of English will not long outlive the technical, commercial, and
military ascendancy of its Anglo-American power base, particularly if a stronger
285 power arises to challenge it. But just because the use of English around the
world might decline does not mean the values associated today with its spread
must also decline. Ultimately, democracy, international trade, and economic
development can flourish in any tongue.

Y Joshua A. Fishman is Emeritus Distinguished University Research Professor
290 (Social Sciences) at Yeshiva University and visiting professor at Stanford
University (Linguistics and Language Learning and Planning) and New York
University (Educational Psychology).

Source: Fishman, J. A. (1998). The new linguistic order. *Foreign Policy*, 113, 26–39.

58